"Finally! A textbook on the sociology of emotions conceptualized and written exclusively for an undergraduate audience. Scott Harris has filled an enormous gap with this accessible overview of the most interesting concepts, provocative findings, and latest research in the study of emotions. Replete with timely examples and infused with humor, students who accept Harris' invitation will be richly rewarded for doing so!"

John R. Mitrano, Sociology,
Central Connecticut State University

"With its clear writing and relevant everyday examples, *An Invitation to the Sociology of Emotions* is a highly accessible way for students to engage the core concepts from Hochschild's and others' work. This concise textbook provides a sociology-of-emotions lens through which students can view the self, interaction, and society in a new light."

Jennifer Lois, Sociology,
Western Washington University

"Scott Harris has identified a problem facing anyone attempting to teach—or learn about—the sociology of emotions: the lack of material aimed at beginners. *An Invitation to the Sociology of Emotions* solves that problem. Instructors and students alike will appreciate its clear presentation of concepts and theories, its accessible language, and its use of examples from recent research in the field."

Leslie Irvine, Sociology,
University of Colorado, Boulder

"Scott Harris gives a grand tour through the sociology of emotions, expertly engaging readers with fascinating topics, insightful theory, and pivotal foundations for understanding social interactions. With its welcoming and practical prose, *An Invitation to the Sociology of Emotions* will serve as a valuable resource for faculty and students."

Nancy Berns, Sociology, Drake University, and
author of *Closure: The Rush to End Grief and What It Costs Us*

"Although positioned as reading for beginners, *An Invitation to the Sociology of Emotions* surpasses a regular textbook in intention, scope, depth, and professional enthusiasm. The second edition promises to be even more interesting, as it reflects new research on social media and provides refinements to the concepts of emotional norms and emotion management strategies."

Olga A. Simonova, Sociology, HSE University,
translator of *An Invitation to the Sociology of Emotions* into Russian

An Invitation to the Sociology of Emotions

Unique in its approach, *An Invitation to the Sociology of Emotions* treats neophytes as its primary audience, giving students a brief, but thorough, introduction to the sociology of emotions. Including research examples, exercises, and lists of further reading, this text explains as clearly as possible some of the most interesting theoretical concepts that animate sociological research on emotions. In this new edition, the author updates the volume with recent research on emotion management, emotional labor, and emotions in social media.

Scott R. Harris, PhD, is a professor of Sociology at Saint Louis University. He is the author of *How to Critique Journal Articles in the Social Sciences* (2nd Ed.) and, with Kathy Charmaz and Leslie Irvine, *The Social Self and Everyday Life: Understanding the World through Symbolic Interactionism*. He also co-edited (with Joel Best) *Making Sense of Social Problems* and co-authored (with Kerry Ferris) *Stargazing: Celebrity, Fame, and Social Interaction*. He is past editor-in-chief of the journals *Symbolic Interaction* and *Sociology Compass*.

An Invitation to the Sociology of Emotions

Second Edition

Scott R. Harris

NEW YORK AND LONDON

Designed cover image: © Shutterstock #676582237, Castleski

Second edition published 2024
by Routledge
605 Third Avenue, New York, NY 10158

and by Routledge
4 Park Square, Milton Park, Abingdon, Oxon, OX14 4RN

Routledge is an imprint of the Taylor & Francis Group, an informa business

© 2024 Scott R. Harris

The right of Scott R. Harris to be identified as author of this work has been asserted in accordance with sections 77 and 78 of the Copyright, Designs and Patents Act 1988.

All rights reserved. No part of this book may be reprinted or reproduced or utilised in any form or by any electronic, mechanical, or other means, now known or hereafter invented, including photocopying and recording, or in any information storage or retrieval system, without permission in writing from the publishers.

Trademark notice: Product or corporate names may be trademarks or registered trademarks and are used only for identification and explanation without intent to infringe.

First edition published by Routledge 2015

Library of Congress Cataloging-in-Publication Data
Names: Harris, Scott R., 1969 September 16– author.
Title: An invitation to the sociology of emotions / Scott R. Harris.
Description: 2nd edition. | New York, NY : Routledge, 2024. |
Includes bibliographical references and index.
Identifiers: LCCN 2023042872 | ISBN 9781032474168 (hardback) |
ISBN 9781032474151 (paperback) | ISBN 9781003386025 (ebook)
Subjects: LCSH: Emotions–Social aspects. | Social psychology.
Classification: LCC HM1033 .H385 2024 | DDC 302–dc23/eng/20230927
LC record available at https://lccn.loc.gov/2023042872

ISBN: 978-1-032-47416-8 (hbk)
ISBN: 978-1-032-47415-1 (pbk)
ISBN: 978-1-003-38602-5 (ebk)

DOI: 10.4324/b23334

Typeset in Galliard
by Newgen Publishing UK

Contents

Note for Instructors		*viii*
Acknowledgements		*xi*
1	Thinking Sociologically about Emotions	1
2	Emotion Norms	13
3	Emotion Management	31
4	Exchanging Emotions	48
5	Emotional Labor	60
6	Identifying Emotions	81
7	Why Study the Sociology of Emotions?	101
	Bibliography	*108*
	Index	*123*

Note for Instructors

This textbook invites students to explore the sociology of emotions, a field that was launched by Hochschild's (1983) groundbreaking book *The Managed Heart*. Like many instructors, I have frequently assigned *The Managed Heart* in class and have highly recommended it to others. It's brilliant and provocative and has informed the work of hundreds of emotion scholars. On the other hand, it is challenging to read and becoming a bit dated.

Hochschild (understandably) wrote for other scholars first, and secondarily for lay and student readers. For example, her chapter on "Paying Respects with Feeling" skips right over the basics of exchange theory in order to discuss nuanced differences between improvised and straight exchanges. As a result, *The Managed Heart* serves researchers well but not entry-level audiences.

In contrast, *An Invitation to the Sociology of Emotions* takes beginners as its primary audience. My goal is to explain as clearly and engagingly as possible the theoretical concepts that animate *The Managed Heart* and the research it has inspired. I am tempted to describe my book as a Cliffs Notes version of Hochschild's book. That analogy is only partly correct though, as my book incorporates scores of examples and updates from research published in the past four decades. Scholars of emotional labor have made important correctives and additions to Hochschild's argument. Moreover, I devote a full chapter to the topic of labeling emotions, a subject relegated to a short appendix in *The Managed Heart*.

Readers should note that my book is titled "An Invitation" and not "An Introduction." In academic parlance, an *introduction* is usually a systematic summary, an elementary overview of a field that may span 300–500 hundred pages. In contrast, an *invitation* is a request to take part in an activity. An invitation is meant to be enticing; it alludes to what's to come without giving too much away. That is the purpose of this book—to ignite students' interest in the sociology of emotions. The scope is not comprehensive. The length is very short, and the price more affordable. However, that means instructors teaching an entire course on emotion will need to supplement this book with additional readings. Those who adopt the book as a supplement for other courses (such as Introduction to Sociology or Social Psychology) might augment the book with a few articles, perhaps taken from the suggested readings at the end of each chapter.

In 2005, Turner and Stets published an impressive 350-page tome entitled *The Sociology of Emotions*—a more thorough summary of a wide range of perspectives on emotion. Their book remains an outstanding resource for researchers and graduate students. However, Turner and Stet's (2005:317) goal was to encourage *scholars* to develop "a more general and robust sociological theory of emotions." In contrast, *An Invitation to the Sociology of Emotions* is intended to be used as a vehicle for capturing the interest of readers who may have no idea what sociology is, let alone a desire to aid in its theoretical development.

I want to introduce non-specialists to a small sampling of the most interesting concepts from the sociology of emotions. My students have found that these concepts shine a fascinating light on their own lives and the world around them. Most of them have no interest in becoming professional sociologists, yet they appreciate the way sociological insights on emotion can illuminate their personal relationships as well as their current jobs and future career paths—in medicine, counseling, business, law, education, and other realms.

All the chapters (except the introduction and conclusion) provide exercises that encourage students to "test out" the applicability of the concepts. Instructors may use these exercises as prompts for class discussions or as short written assignments. Enterprising instructors may combine the exercises into a larger term paper that requires students to apply class ideas to real or hypothetical examples of their choosing.

The first six chapters conclude with annotated lists of suggested readings that can be used in a variety of ways. Instructors may recommend or require that the entire class reads some of them; or, particular students (individually or in groups) may be assigned to report on certain readings, either verbally or in writing. Alternatively, instructors may choose to use the readings as lecture material and summarize the content for students. Lastly, some of the readings may be incorporated into a larger term paper assignment, along with the exercises.

The second edition has been updated throughout. Most importantly, I added discussions of social media—texting, emailing, Facebook, Instagram, TikTok, Twitter, and the like—to six of the chapters. Two of the boxed Spotlights on Research are new (in Chapter 2 and Chapter 6). I incorporated references to approximately 50 additional articles and books, with an emphasis on recent examples and research. Most of these sources can be found in the reference section, but some are in the suggested readings found at the ends of Chapters 1–6.

Using the first edition in class for several years gave me the opportunity to locate ambiguities, mistakes, omissions, and several embarrassing typos, which I've attempted to correct. The second edition now includes a discussion of rule reminders (Chapter 2); a fleshed-out treatment of surface acting via facial expressions (Chapter 3); improved discussion of emotions as the outputs vs. inputs of exchange calculations (Chapter 4); clarification regarding whether workplace slogans ("The customer is always right") can be used to encourage deep vs. surface acting, and whether sociologists tend to be primarily concerned with social justice or with helping workers perform better in their jobs (Chapter 5); a definition of upgrading and downgrading emotional labels, and an explanation of the overlap between surface acting and emotional identification (Chapter 6); and so on. References to popular culture have been expanded and in some cases updated (rest-in-peace to Joan Rivers and the Tea Party, hello to Jennifer Lawrence and the MAGA movement). To make the book more student friendly, I've added numbers to those all headings that were parts of lists, such as "Five Surface Acting Strategies."

Acknowledgements

Thanks go to my students Ruth Bouman and Lauren Pendergast, who helped me with popular culture references and other useful advice after they read the first edition in class. My college dean, Donna LaVoie, was exceptionally kind and supportive when I reached the limit of what I could do as a faculty member. I appreciate her patience during my personal encounter with the Peter Principle. Candace Clark (who helped launch the sociology of emotions in the 1980s) took me under her wing during my first conference in 1994 and in subsequent conversations. I am still grateful for her encouragement, without which I may not have published my first article or taught my first class on emotion, both in 1997. My graduate school officemate, Phil Zuckerman, wrote a clear, concise, engaging, and informative book (*Invitation to the Sociology of Religion*) which served as an exemplar for me—as did the classic *Invitation to Sociology* by Peter Berger. Finally, my biggest thanks go to Jenine Harris, my favorite person for the last thirty years.

I appreciate the helpful comments provided by the reviewers:

- Nancy Berns   Drake University
- John R. Mitrano   Central Connecticut State University
- Jennifer Lois   Western Washington University
- Nathan Rousseau   Jacksonville University

1 Thinking Sociologically about Emotions

What do you think when you hear the phrase "the sociology of emotions"? Such a topic may never have occurred to you before. The key terms—*sociology* and *emotions*—may seem a nebulous and unlikely pairing.

Nevertheless, there is a vibrant tradition of research on this topic that many people find fascinating, illuminating, and useful. Especially since the publication of Arlie Hochschild's (1983) influential book *The Managed Heart*, hundreds of scholars have made contributions to the sociological study of emotions. By examining some preconceptions you may have—and perhaps overcoming some of them—then perhaps you too will become intrigued by the concepts, arguments, and findings of this subfield.

So, let's take a look at seven assumptions that can impede an enthusiastic engagement with the literature on the sociology of emotions. Sociologists tend to challenge these preconceptions in their research. I'll explain how they do so and will outline the subsequent chapters of this book at the same time.

1. Are Emotions Trivial? (No, They Are Pervasive and Crucial)

Human behavior is often compartmentalized into three categories: people think, they act, and they feel. Studies of thoughts and actions need no justification; they are considered respectable and important topics in their own right. Feeling, in contrast, is suspect. Among Americans at least, emotion is often derogated and treated as inferior. When I tell people that I'm teaching a course on emotion, they sometimes look at me askance. They wonder if my class will be "touchy-feely" rather than rigorous or scientific. A friend of mine—a high school history teacher—burst out laughing when I told him I was teaching a course on emotion. He seemed to think that classes would consist primarily of students sharing their feelings and giving each other hugs.

Compared to the subject of emotions, other class titles have a greater aura of importance. Who would scoff at a college-level course on poverty, unemployment, crime, or terrorism? The real and perceived harms that are associated with these social problems generate a certain respectability and seriousness. Few would doubt that these topics matter.

DOI: 10.4324/b23334-1

At first glance, the topic of emotions seems less serious and significant. That is a major preconception that can prevent people from reading and learning from sociological research on the topic. All of the chapters that follow will address the charge of triviality, as there are important and useful concepts in each of them. For now, I will make just two simple points.

One way to challenge the preconception that emotions are trivial is to highlight the fact that *emotions are pervasive*. Even if emotions are "softer" or less serious than other topics—an assumption I don't agree with—then we could at least say that emotions warrant study because they pervade our lives so thoroughly. If I followed you around for a day, do you think I would find that emotions played a big role in your life? Would I find you saying "I'm so bored" or "That was exciting!" or "My friend is irritating me" or even "I love ice cream"? Then, add to these examples the feelings that you think about or experience but don't articulate: the flash of frustration at a long line, the bit of amusement that a tweet or TikTok video gives you, the nervousness you feel when taking an exam or getting ready for a date or being pulled over by a police officer. Then, add to those examples the emotions that you provoke in others—the sympathy, jealousy, exasperation, embarrassment, and other feelings that you rouse through the things you say or do.

Simple reflection and casual observation tell us that our everyday experiences are saturated with emotions. It's hard to imagine living our lives without them. Surely, such a phenomenon deserves some of our time and attention, doesn't it?

A second response to the charge of triviality is to note that emotions are inextricably connected to virtually any "larger" issue that people deem consequential and important. Unemployment is not simply about a lack of financial resources; it is also a problem because of the associated negative feelings—insecurity and worry over bills; lowered self-esteem due to loss of identity; embarrassment at revealing one's status to others; depression after failed attempts to find meaningful work. Crime, too, is inextricably connected to emotions—from the "sneaky thrills" of vandalism and petty theft, to the sense of community and pride that may come from gang identity, to the righteous anger that motivates violence after a perceived insult, attack, or injustice (Katz 1988; Scheff 1994; Loseke 2009). More positive feelings and behaviors should not be overlooked as well. Love, affection, sympathy, gratitude, respect—these and other emotions help us maintain relationships, communities, and even nations. Succinctly put, emotions are "essential for forming and perpetuating human societies" (Clark 2002:155).

Clearly, emotions are not trivial. They are a pervasive and fundamental part of our daily lives. They give color and meaning to virtually all our experiences—from the most mundane to the most extraordinary situations. Although they are often portrayed as less interesting or important than thinking and acting, emotions are intricately connected to our daily thoughts and behaviors. They sustain or threaten our most valued relationships and identities.

2. Are Emotions Exclusively or Primarily Biological? (No, They Are Highly Social)

A second obstacle to the sociological study of emotions is the idea that emotions are primarily biological phenomena. This is a tempting assumption to make. As William James (1884) might say, what is an emotion if it is not something that is *felt*? It is hard to imagine being "intensely angry" without experiencing any physiological changes—such as an increased heart rate, elevated skin temperature, or a general sense of being "worked up." Try to imagine yourself saying "I am so upset right now" in a flat, monotone, robotic voice. Emotions often seem undeniably connected to our bodies.

Compelling evolutionary arguments can be made that emotions have a genetic basis (Al-Shawaf and Lewis 2017; Turner 2011). Like claws, stripes, and other anatomical features, emotions play a key role in natural selection, or "the survival of the fittest." Emotions signal information to other animals—as when a cat puffs up its fur, bares its fangs, and hisses in order to tell a predator or competitor to "backoff." At the same time, emotions can prepare an animal to act: the ability to fight or flee is aided by the adrenaline, the increased heart rate, and other physiological states that accompany particular emotions.

Some argue that people, like animals, are genetically programmed to experience and display certain emotions. Fear in the face of danger; jealousy when a romantic partner flirts with another; love when looking at the face of one's newborn child—these emotions and others can be portrayed as evolutionary products and primarily physiological.

While not necessarily denying that emotions have some sort of biological basis, sociologists tend to emphasize *the social dimensions of emotions*. One way to clarify the difference is to recall the popular distinction between "nature" and "nurture." Are emotions primarily innate or are we socialized into particular ways of experiencing and expressing emotions? Most sociologists tend to emphasize the latter in their studies. As Clark (2002:163) put it, "Just because emotional equipment is built in does not mean that humans have no control over it."

For example, in Chapter 2 we will examine the concept of *emotion norms*. Whereas a biological point of view suggests that our physiology largely dictates our feelings, a sociological point of view suggests that cultural rules govern the emotions that people experience and display.

While attending a funeral, a conversation may strike you as funny or you may be especially pleased to see an old friend. However, normative expectations may require that you maintain a hushed tone of voice and suppress any feelings of amusement or glee. Of course—and as you may already be thinking—this is *not* the norm everywhere! In some settings, such as an Irish wake, participants are encouraged to raise a glass and cheerfully celebrate the life of a departed loved one. Rather than being biologically predetermined, emotion norms vary by culture (Thoits 2004).

Norms are one way (but by no means the only way) that sociologists highlight the social rather than the biological dimensions of human emotions. Chapters 3–6 contain other concepts that either challenge or augment a purely biological perspective on emotions.

3. Are Emotions Automatic and Inevitable? (No, They Are Often Contingent and Malleable)

A third impediment to approaching emotions sociologically is the tendency to treat feelings as automatic or inevitable. This preconception may stem from a biological orientation, but not always. You'll notice this preconception when you hear people say "It's only natural" to feel an emotion—such as intense sadness after the loss of a loved one, annoyance when slowed down by heavy traffic, or jealousy when a spouse spends time with an attractive person. Listen also for proverbs and maxims that suggest an inexorable sequence of emotions and behavior: "The heart wants what the heart wants." Statements that start with "of course"—as in "Of course that pissed me off"—may also exhibit this third preconception.

People often believe or claim that emotional states are things that happen to us, as if we had little or no control over the feelings we experienced. And this notion seems to have an element of truth to it. Probably all of us can remember times when we seemed to be "struck" or burdened by a negative emotion that we could not escape. Stage fright or depression may tenaciously afflict us despite our intense desire to feel something more positive, such as confidence or happiness. Sometimes even medication fails us, and we may feel there is little we can do to prevent or change certain emotions.

However, an overemphasis on the inevitability of emotionality can blind us to all the creative ways that people try—with varying degrees of success—to actively manage emotions in their everyday lives. One of the most studied topics in the sociology of emotions is the strategies people use to modify feelings—their own as well as the feelings of others. In Chapter 3, I'll introduce this tradition of research to you through the concepts of surface acting and deep acting (Hochschild 1983). These concepts highlight the ways people try to control—rather than simply being moved by—their emotions.

Surface acting refers to the strategies people use to manage how they appear to feel. Despite being nervous on a date or at a job interview, we can try to act calm, cool, and collected: we can smile and speak with a confident tone as we describe ourselves as "feeling great." Through these sorts of strategies, people can attempt to shape how they appear to feel to others. Con artists may employ these strategies for ill, but hopefully most of us use them for good reasons.

People don't just modify their outward emotional appearances. On many occasions, individuals attempt to change their inner feelings rather than masking or faking them. *Deep acting* refers to the strategies people use to manage how they actually feel. The most interesting technique is *cognitive* deep acting, which occurs when we change our thoughts on a situation in order to alter our emotional states. Prior to an important job interview, applicants may silently "pump themselves up" by repeating motivational phrases like "Come on! You can do this! You're smart and have an impressive resume!" or calm themselves down by thinking "If it's meant to be, it's meant to be. Just relax and be yourself."

As we'll see in Chapter 5, surface and deep acting are not limited to our private lives. We also use these techniques to manage emotions at our places of work. Waitresses, cashiers, and other customer service representatives—as well as lawyers, doctors, and accountants—all attempt to manage the emotions they experience and present to their customers, co-workers, and employers.

In short, sociological research emphasizes the fact that emotions are much more than automatic or instinctive reactions. Rather, human beings are constantly managing and manipulating how they feel, in order to conform to social norms and negotiate their relationships with others.

4. Are Emotions Irrational? (Not Necessarily—Thought and Emotion Are Intricately Intertwined)

A fourth impediment to approaching emotions sociologically is the popular assumption that feelings are irrational (Clark 2002:155–156). As we mentioned under the first preconception, feelings are often treated as separate and inferior to thinking. Thought is the province of logic and reasoning. Emotions are considered more subjective, mysterious, and whimsical. "Emotions cloud our judgment," people often argue. Moreover, it is often assumed that men are the more logical while women are (at best) more sensitive to their own and others' feelings and (at worst) more prone to emotional hysteria.

As a fan of *Star Trek*—the television shows and movies—it has been amusing to notice how this fourth preconception has shaped scripts and character choices on the show. For example, you might recall that Spock, the science officer on the original TV show, was a half-Vulcan (on his father's side) and half-human (on his mother's side). It was his Vulcan heritage that was portrayed as making Spock such an outstanding scientist, as emotions are "foreign to" (or at least strictly controlled by) that race of people. *Star Trek: The Next Generation* (*ST:TNG*) continued this theme with the character of Data—a male android who was completely incapable of experiencing emotions. His lack of emotional bias was portrayed as making him incredibly astute and speedy thinker (though occasionally exhibiting poor social etiquette). After the TV show ended, an "emotion chip" was installed in Data during the first *ST:TNG* movie. This tended to make Data a much less reliable science officer. The most recent iteration of the franchise—*Star Trek: Enterprise*—abandoned the gendered element but still put a nearly emotionless Vulcan (female) character, T'Pol, in the role of science officer. Whether Vulcans or androids, the common cultural assumption exhibited in these shows was that feelings tend to get in the way of thoughtful analysis. Emotions are deemed irrational or antithetical to thought.

As we'll see in Chapters 2 and 3, sociologists tend to challenge any strict or gendered boundaries between thought and emotion. The concepts of emotion norms and cognitive deep acting both imply a deep connection between thought and emotion, on the parts of both men and women. It takes thought to assess situations and conform to the relevant emotion norms. And, through cognitive deep acting, people shape their feelings by manipulating their thoughts.

Chapter 4 focuses most squarely on the topic of rationality, by applying *exchange theory* to the subject of emotions. According to exchange theory, human beings carefully calculate how much they are putting into and receiving out of any situation. For example, if a neighbor asks you to pick up the mail while they are out of town, you might expect gratitude ("Thanks!") or deference ("You're so nice!"). If you deem the transaction a fair one, then you may repeat it by offering to help again on a later date. However, if the neighbor does not express appreciation and fails to reciprocate when you travel, then you may be much less likely to exchange favors with that person in the future.

Sociologists have expanded this notion to look at how people—in a very "rational" or calculating way—keep track of who is giving and getting what to whom. People trade goods, services, *and* feelings, in formal economic settings and during informal interactions. As Hochschild (1983) argued, people often act as though they possess a "mental ledger" that records the emotions they give to and receive from others. If we have offered sympathy and support to a friend after a difficult break-up, then we may expect to be "paid back" at a later date when we are in need. We also sometimes use emotions to enforce reciprocal exchanges, as when we sanction those who cheat us by shaming them or expressing anger towards them. In all these instances, we are (arguably) being very rational and calculating about feelings that are often assumed to be antithetical to careful thought.

5. Are Emotions Private and Personal? (They Are Created, Managed, and Even Sold in Public Venues)

In a famous song by Tom Petty, the rocker plaintively repeats the chorus "You don't know how it feels. You don't know how it feels… to be me." In her song "Therefore I Am," Billie Eilish sings something similar: "Don't talk 'bout me like how you might know how I feel." Petty and Eilish's sentiments are echoed in many ways through other common phrases used in everyday life. You might have heard people exclaim "You can't imagine how I feel!" or "You have no idea what it feels like to [go through the experience I had]!" People also assert their own ignorance of others' emotions when they assert that "I have no idea what it feels like" to be a mother, to lose a child, or to grow up poor, since they lack personal experience. Taken to its extreme, this preconception can assert a form of solipsism, where each individual's emotional experiences are unique and can never be understood or imagined by others.

Another manifestation of this preconception is the way people treat their emotional troubles as private issues rather than as connected to larger, shared problems. Students, teammates, or employees may wonder "What's wrong with me? Why am I so nervous, lonely, or depressed?" when they could look to the competitive culture of their classroom, league, or workplace. People often turn inward to explain unwanted feelings—as if all emotional troubles were due to a personality defect—when external factors may guide individuals' emotional experiences in somewhat common or patterned ways.

Rather than conceptualizing emotions as solely or mostly private possessions, sociologists emphasize the social dimensions of emotion (McCarthy 1989; 2021). As Chapter 2 will explain, emotion norms are culturally shared expectations that govern individuals' feelings—and people's reactions to those feelings. Emotional labor, as we'll see in Chapter 5, is a decidedly public endeavor wherein people are paid to produce company-preferred emotional states. A worker's emotions can be monitored by her employers, co-workers, and customers, to ensure that "appropriate" feelings are experienced and displayed. A customer service representative who exhibits too much anger, frustration, or sadness may find themselves sanctioned via small tips from customers, disparaging comments from co-workers, or pink slips from employers.

To be sure, our companions may not be "correct" in their assessments of our feelings, but that does not stop them from monitoring us and issuing us rewards and sanctions as they see fit. Thus, as we'll see in multiple chapters, our emotional states are regularly treated as public entities—even commodities—even though there is often a popular assumption that they are private possessions.

6. Are Emotions Indescribable? (People Actively Discuss and Label Feelings on a Daily Basis)

The fifth preconception asserted that feelings are "mine and mine alone—no one can tell me how I feel." In an interesting twist, the sixth preconception asserts that even an individual undergoing an emotional state cannot tell others what they are feeling. A common claim in American society is that our most important feelings are indescribable. The idea is that some feelings are so big or so overwhelming that no word or sentence could do them justice. "My love for you is beyond words" a romantic suitor may assert. Or, people say "I can't tell you how upset [or happy] that makes me," once again claiming that a sentiment is so powerful that it is too much for our verbal skills to handle.

One example that you might be able to find on YouTube.com comes from the ninth season of the TV show *American Idol*. The winner that year was rocker Lee DeWise. After months of hard work, intense competition, and public performances, the season culminated in a huge success for

DeWise—he'd won first place and garnered millions of fans. DeWise had gone from obscurity to fame in less than a year. On the final episode, DeWise stood in front of an adoring crowd when host Ryan Seacrest announced his victory for the first time. After the thunderous applause finally quieted, Seacrest asked "What did it feel like when I said your name?" You might imagine several potential descriptors that DeWise could have used: elation, joy, nervousness, surprise, excitement, relief, and others. Instead, DeWise claimed "there are no words." Similarly, Jennifer Hudson (also a former *American Idol* contestant) released a 2014 album with the song "I Can't Describe (the Way I Feel)." In it she tells a romantic partner "I just can't put in words what I feel for you."

If taken to its extreme, this preconception could lead us to ask: Why study emotions? What could be learned about a phenomenon about which people cannot speak? If people can't describe their deepest, most meaningful emotions, then should the topic perhaps be left to the realms of melody, art, sexuality, or other symbolic gestures?

Despite occasions of apparent ineffability, people regularly do label their own emotions—quite routinely in fact, and on important occasions too (Harris and Ferris 2009). In Chapter 6, we'll look at the social factors that shape how people assign labels to feelings—their own and those of others. When someone says "I'm happy to be here," that "My mom absolutely loves President Zelensky [of Ukraine]," or that a group of protesters is "an angry mob," these statements all can be analyzed as strategic arguments that make particular impressions on audiences and accomplish certain goals. A politician may claim he is "thrilled" to be at a debate, but there is a good chance that his audience's expectations and his goal of winning over voters could be shaping his use of that particular label rather than another one (such as nervous or annoyed).

Interactional audiences and objectives are two social factors that shape how we label or identify our emotions. Another is the vocabulary we are taught to use. As we'll see in Chapter 6, not all cultures share the same emotion vocabulary (Heelas 1986). For example, Samoans use a single word (*alofa*) to refer to liking, love, and sympathy, and they do not differentiate hate from disgust (Russell 1989:296). On the other hand, the Utku[1] make finer distinctions than Americans do, employing separate terms for fear of physical harm (*iqhi*) and fear of being treated unkindly (*ilira*); they also coined a term (*qiquq*) to describe "being on the verge of tears because of bottled-up hostility" (Russell 1989:294). People are encouraged to use different sets of categories to describe their feelings, depending on the language they speak as well as the occupations they hold. Some employees may be instructed to say how "proud" they are of their company's products and services, how much they "really care" about their customers, or how "sorry" they feel for their competitors, even if (at least on some occasions) the workers might prefer to describe themselves differently.

In short, despite a preconception that Americans sometimes have—that emotions are ineffable—people regularly do discuss and label their emotions, both weak and strong ones. Consequently, sociologists can study the social processes, settings, and vocabularies that shape how the labeling occurs.

In recent decades, the internet, smartphones, and other technological advancements have enabled us to interact via email, text, tweet, posts on discussion forums, and other kinds of computer mediated communication. Online platforms offer new opportunities and constraints for expressing ourselves—what scholars call "digital affordances" (Bareither 2019). Many people now have easy access to emojis, stickers, GIFs, and other images that we can quickly insert into our messages. As a result, we increasingly depict feelings visually—for example, by including a smiley or angry face rather than only relying on prose. These visual ways of characterizing emotions can also be analyzed as social practices, as Chapter 6 will discuss.

7. Do Emotions Belong Solely to the Realm of Psychology? (No, Sociologists and Other Social Scientists Can Make Valuable Contributions)

Compared to other subjects, sociology is not taught much in high schools. For most students, exposure to this discipline happens in college, if at all. If any social science discipline comes to mind in connection to emotion, it is likely to be psychology, which is more frequently taught in American high schools (and more commonly discussed on television and in film). Moreover, because of psychology's greater emphasis on the individual and on human anatomy—as well as its connection to psychiatry and counseling—emotions seem at first glance to fit most comfortably in that discipline.

Despite this preconception, social scientists from many different disciplines have been studying feelings for decades. Faculty members in departments of anthropology, communication, geography, history, and sociology have conducted interesting research on emotions. Anyone who studies human beings may develop an interest in emotions, since they are crucial to human behavior and social problems. Thus, you may need to reconsider some preconceptions you may have about boundaries between the social sciences. There is much overlap in their purviews or "turf." Emotions can and should be examined from a number of perspectives; it seems risky to presume that one discipline has a monopoly on the truth.

In the following six chapters, I will draw on multiple disciplines but will focus primarily on what sociologists have written about emotions. I think that sociologists have a great deal to contribute to this topic, given the incredible breadth and depth of their interest in the social factors that impinge upon the human experience. My goal is to provide a lively and clear guidebook. The emphasis will be on concepts that readers can "test out" in their everyday lives, with less prominence given to specific research findings that must be memorized.

As my title indicates, I've written an *invitation* to this sociological subfield, not a comprehensive treatment of it. I have focused on those ideas that my students have found most interesting, accessible, and applicable. After finishing this book, readers can look to other sources (such as those recommended at the end of each chapter) for more technical examples and comprehensive summaries of what sociologists have written about emotions.

What Are Emotions?

Usually the first chapter of a textbook must admit how difficult it is to define social phenomena. Even the smartest scholars can't articulate *exactly* what their work is about. There is no easy or perfect way to define concepts like altruism, culture, family, globalization, prejudice, religion, sports, terrorism, or white-collar crime (see Harris 2022, ch. 3). Social life is so messy—and so interesting—that it frequently evades straightforward descriptions. As a result, different scholars often propose somewhat idiosyncratic definitions of key terms, depending on their theoretical and methodological preferences.

The subject of emotions follows the same tendency. Social scientists have not settled on a single "best way" to conceptualize exactly what emotions are. In the 1980s and early 1990s, scholars articulated more than twenty different definitions for the concept of emotion (van Brakel 1994), and no consensus has been reached since then[2] (Izard 2010; Ortony 2022). Some definitions are relatively succinct and minimalist: "Emotions are responses to situations interpreted on the basis of previous social learning" (Clanton 1989:179). Other definitions are much longer and packed with dense meanings: "An emotion is a universal, functional reaction to an external stimulus event, temporarily integrating physiological, cognitive, phenomenological, and behavioral channels to facilitate a fitness-enhancing, environment-shaping response to the current situation" (Kalat and Shiota 2007:313).

In sociology, probably the most well-known definition comes from Hochschild (1983:17, 219). In her view, emotions are a biological *sense*, similar to sight, hearing, and smell. Like these senses, emotions provide us with information about the world and prepare us for action. Fear, for example, indicates danger while an increased heart rate prepares us to flee or fight. On the other hand, Hochschild argued, emotions are also tied to our perspectives. Feelings can be treated as *clues* to how we are thinking or how others are thinking. For example, a parent may feel proud of a child who is starring in the lead role of a school play. The pride (as a sense) is providing information about what is happening in the world: the parent's child is doing well. At the same time, the emotion can be treated as a clue to the parent's socially acquired perspective: perhaps the child's success is being interpreted as a sign of effective parenting.

Some emotions may at first seem strictly biological or automatic but can still be treated as clues to our perspectives on things (see Hochschild 1983:221). For example, fear in the face of death seems "only natural." However, fear can be shaped and colored by fervent beliefs in the existence of an afterlife, in the value of an individual's life as opposed to a larger cause, and other cultural factors. Certainly, the feelings people experience when delayed by freeway traffic can be treated as clues to their perspectives: the level of frustration depends on one's expectations for "how things should work for this time of day," the value one places on time in the car (compared to TV-time or computer-time), and other considerations.

Hochschild's definition—that emotions are linked (like a sense) to what is going on in the world and (like a clue) to what is going on in our heads—has seemed to work well enough for many sociologists. Some of the concepts that will appear in this book (such as *cognitive deep acting*, *burnout*, and *ambivalence*) stem directly from Hochschild's definition. However, other ideas (including parts of Chapter 6) require a more agnostic stance about the "true" definition of emotion.

In this book, I will not settle on a single definition, and I encourage readers to do the same. Those who decide to read more books and articles in this area can and should periodically revisit the issue of "how to define emotion." I also encourage readers not to become too flustered by the fact that social scientists (and human beings in general) routinely use words that defy simple definition. If you insist on articulating a perfect definition, then you may become fixated on the pursuit of a mirage that will never materialize.

Notes

1 The Utku live in the Canadian Arctic. See also Briggs (1970).
2 Definition of terms that fall under the umbrella of emotion—such as affect, sentiments, moods, anger, jealousy, and so on—endure the same fate; this includes the category "basic emotions," which are sometimes considered biologically fundamental (Ortony 2022). It is difficult to find any social science concepts whose definitions do not suffer from some degree of arbitrariness and inconsistent usage, as well as the dilemma of infinite regress (where the words used in a definition also need to be defined). See Harris (2022, ch. 3) as well as Dixon (2012) and van Brakel (1994).

Suggested Readings

An Invitation to the Sociology of Emotions attempts to provide a clear and engaging primer. After reading this book, some students may want to consult texts by sociologists that are a bit more challenging, such as the following:

Hochschild, Arlie Russell. 1983. *The Managed Heart*. Berkeley, CA: University of California Press.

Stets, Jan E. and Jonathan H. Turner. 2005. *The Sociology of Emotions*. New York: Cambridge University Press.

Stets, Jan E. and Jonathan H. Turner (eds.). 2014. *Handbook of the Sociology of Emotions* (Vol. II). New York: Springer.

As I mentioned in this chapter, various disciplines have studied emotions from their own particular (yet overlapping) perspectives. For example, anthropologists, geographers, historians, communication scholars, and especially psychologists have all conducted interesting research, as shown in the examples below.

Beatty, Andrew. 2019. *Emotional Worlds: Beyond an Anthropology of Emotion*. Cambridge, UK: Cambridge University Press.

Davidson, Joyce, Liz Bondi, and Mick Smith (eds.). [2006] 2016. *Emotional Geographies*. New York: Routledge.

Dixon, Thomas. 2023. *The History of Emotions: A Very Short Introduction*. New York: Oxford University Press.

Metts, Sandra and Sally Planalp. 2011. "Emotional Experience and Expression." Ch. 9 in *The Sage Handbook of Interpersonal Communication*. 4th Ed. Edited by Mark L. Knapp and John A. Daly. Thousand Oaks, CA: Sage.

Shiota, Michelle N. and James W. Kalat. 2018. *Emotion*. 3rd Ed. New York: Oxford University Press. (Psychological in orientation)

2 Emotion Norms

To take a first step towards a sociological understanding of emotions, let's start with one of the most popular concepts in sociology: social norms. Even if you have not enrolled in a single course in sociology, you probably have some exposure to this concept, which has made its way into public awareness.

Social norms are cultural expectations for how people should behave in particular situations. People are socialized into particular patterns of behavior, which they often come to understand as the "best"—the most "natural," "logical," or "moral"—courses of action. These norms govern nearly everything we do—the clothes we wear, the food we eat, and even what is considered acceptable to look at (Goffman 1963; Rigney 2001).

Imagine a male high school student who wears skirts to class, eats insects for lunch, and strictly avoids making eye contact with teachers. The young man could have a rough life. He will likely receive ill treatment—gossip, looks of disapproval, teasing, ostracism, or even physical attacks—from his classmates, many of whom would likely be quite confident that the student was doing things "wrong." Even close friends might ask, "What's your 'damage'? Why are you so shy around our teachers? Why do you dress like a girl? Your lunch is disgusting—you're sick, dude!" Of course, any of these classmates think the way they do because of the socialization they have received. If they had been raised in another culture, they would be equally confident that boys can wear skirts (e.g., kilts), that worm tacos and chocolate covered grasshoppers are nutritious and delicious, or that avoiding eye contact is an appropriate sign of deference to one's superiors.

The concept of *emotion norms* is an extension of the concept of social norms; it can be defined as cultural expectations regarding how people should feel in particular situations; or, socially acquired standards for assessing the appropriateness of emotions that we experience and display (Thoits 2004). For example, a high school student who cries after he receives a "B" on a relatively small homework assignment, or who laughs gleefully whenever he understands the point of a teacher's lesson, might be deemed emotionally deviant by his peers.

DOI: 10.4324/b23334-2

Let's examine some basic features of emotion norms, so you can better understand the concept and more carefully apply it to your own experiences and to the world around you.

Six Features of Emotion Norms

1) Emotion Norms Are Pervasive, Yet Often Invisible

It can be difficult to start looking for social norms, because we usually don't notice them. When a friend talks A LITTLE TOO LOUDLY or standsalittletooclose—that's when you realize that you and your companions are conforming to subtle expectations to which you hadn't given much thought.

The same is true of emotion norms. When someone thanks us for a small favor, we may barely notice. Yet there may a "deafening silence" when expected gratitude does not arrive. If you've ever held open a door for a group of people who neglect to even acknowledge your existence, then you might know what I mean. Emotion norms "become visible in those moments when they are violated" (Davis 2012:34). Similarly, expressions of envy must be handled with extreme caution. A friend who routinely tells us "I wish I had your good looks!" might commit an uncomfortable violation of the widespread rule against covetous sentiments (Clanton 2006), unless perhaps the statement was imbued with a whimsical rather than begrudging tone.

Sometimes we become implicitly aware of emotion norms when we realize that our own feelings are at risk of being deviant. As Hochschild (1983:57) argued, people may experience a "pinch" when there is a mismatch between what they feel and what they are expected to feel. For example, at many New Year's Eve parties, the norm is that people will cheer, smile, blow horns, and hug the people around them once the clock strikes midnight. Partygoers who have lethargic or pessimistic attitudes about the passage of time, or trepidation about being affectionate with others, are not likely to fit in to the emotional tone of the gathering (Hochschild 1979:564). Consequently, they may give themselves a silent reminder of the rules: "Come on! You should be enjoying this!" Their companions may tell them something similar, out loud: "Don't be such a downer!" Hochschild (1983:57–58) argues that this is evidence for the existence of emotion norms: we know norms exist (in part) because people give these kinds of *rule reminders* to others and to themselves, at times when misfitting feelings are noticed.

Because emotion norms are usually taken for granted, it can be difficult to spot them. The more you practice, however, the easier it is to apply this concept. The trick is to (a) pick a specific setting or social interaction and (b) imagine an emotional reaction (or observe a real one) that would seem either inappropriate, immoral, or culturally "illogical" to most of the people you know.

2) Emotion Norms Are Enforced by Our Companions and by Ourselves, Via Major and Minor Sanctions

Police officers issue sanctions—such as a speeding ticket—when they catch us violating rules of the road. These sanctions serve as a punishment and a deterrent to breaking the law. In a similar but less formal fashion, *interactional policing* also occurs when it comes to implicit rules governing emotions.

Our companions can use a variety of strategies to enforce social and emotional norms (see Berger 1963, ch. 4). People may give us dirty looks or disapproving comments; they may damage our reputations by gossiping about us. Ostracism is an extremely powerful sanction that can be employed. A person who is deemed "too nervous" or "never happy" may have trouble making friends, finding a spouse, or maintaining close ties with kin. Or, someone who expresses inappropriate feelings online might be banned, blocked, unfollowed, or deleted (Crabtree and Richards 2021). Lastly, economic pressures can be brought to bear. Emotional deviance can result in bleaker employment prospects or being financially "cut off" by one's family. An ill-timed display of an inappropriate feeling—anxiety, frustration, or even comedic amusement—might undermine an otherwise successful job interview.

In one well-known study, Simon, Eder, and Evans (1992) observed (over a three-year period) the development of emotion norms among adolescent girls in a Midwestern middle school. The researchers found that young women used teasing, gossip, and confrontations to socialize each other into "appropriate" feelings, such as "One should have romantic feelings only for someone of the opposite sex" and "One should not have romantic feelings for a boy who is already attached." Displays of same-sex affection (e.g., playfully sitting on a friend's lap) could be met with gentle mockery: "You're really not my type" or a chorus of "Oooohs" that teasingly implied a homosexual intent. Girls whose physical appearance or behavior seemed to indicate a lack of interest in boys were called queer or gay or tomboys (in derogatory tones). Romantic feelings for boys were more encouraged. Sometimes, multiple members of a peer group openly discussed their collective attraction to a particular boy. However, as soon as one group member actively pursued or formed a relationship with that boy, none of her friends could continue to express affection for him, without being sanctioned.

In adult settings, emotional deviance can have ramifications as well. For example, a suspect's "nervous" courtroom testimony may be interpreted by juries as a sign of lying; a reserved or detached demeanor, on the other hand, might be viewed as a lack of remorse or conscience. Victims who emote disproportionately to an event—appearing underwhelmed by a serious crime or overwhelmed by a minor crime—may be viewed less favorably by a jury (Rose, Nadler, and Clark 2006). Or, imagine a financial advisor who expressed envy at the large sums of money his or her clients possessed: "Wow, I wish my retirement accounts were as large as yours! You are a lucky bum to inherit money like that." Advisors who blatantly violated norms against expressing envy might cause some clients to question their trustworthiness as well as their etiquette. Such a worker might lose business quickly or at least gain fewer word-of-mouth referrals (Delaney 2012).

Interestingly, it is not only others who monitor and sanction our emotional conduct; we punish ourselves as well. Exhortations to "Get your act together!" can come from ourselves as well as our friends, co-workers, and relatives (Hochschild 1983:57; Thoits 1985). For example, when I graduated from college, my recently divorced parents took me, my siblings, and a few friends out to lunch. I was a bit unnerved by the awkward situation, and just wanted the event to be over. Later on, I realized that my parents had probably been expecting me to make a "toast" or short speech thanking them for the financial sacrifices they had made to put me through school. I then felt guilty and said to myself "Well, that was a dumb thing to forget to do!" My thoughts and feelings can be seen as self-imposed sanctions—as punishments and deterrents to similar behavior in the future. My negative emotions led me to write special "thank-you" cards to my parents, in an attempt to make restitution and convey my gratitude.

3) Emotion Norms Are Learned through Direct and Indirect Socialization

It is tempting to treat emotion norms as simply natural or logical patterns of behavior. Some emotional displays may seem like an obvious or inevitable choice: "of course" a college graduate should express gratitude for their parents' financial assistance. Yet, to recognize the normative aspect of emotional conduct, try this trick: imagine a group of people who might have a different "of course" perspective. In this case, you might picture a wealthy family where paying for a child's education is considered a routine obligation or duty, rather than an optional and significant sacrifice. Among this hypothetical group of people, perhaps a graduate would not be expected to make a grand or public expression of gratitude to his parents—describing their help as a financial "sacrifice" might even be offensive in elite settings.

To further clarify the cultural dimension of emotion norms, let's draw an analogy from social norms about nudity and gender. On a hot summer day, young children can be seen playing in various states of undress. In most neighborhoods in the U.S., swim trunks provide enough coverage for kids to run through the sprinklers or play "tag." Yet at some point, children learn to become self-conscious about nudity. This applies even more so to the girls, for whom going "shirtless" becomes much more taboo. When a girl is closer to six years old rather than three, her parents might tell her that she's a "big girl now" and must wear a top, unlike her brothers. This would constitute *direct socialization*: when others explicitly tell us what the norms are. Alternatively, a young girl may not need any explicit instruction; she may merely look around and notice that none of the older girls, nor any grown women, appear topless in public. This would be *indirect socialization*: when others implicitly inform us what the norms are.

To some Americans, these clothing standards may seem natural, inevitable, or simply "logical." They are not. Some cultures have no taboo regarding bared female breasts, whereas others institute even stricter norms that require the covering of legs, arms, and heads. The rules are social creations, but we internalize them, treating artificial conventions as the way things simply are or ought to be (Berger 1963, ch. 5).

As with norms about nudity, socialization into emotion norms can occur directly or indirectly (and there is often a grey area between the two). Some statements seem to constitute explicit instruction about the feelings that a culture (or subculture) deems appropriate:

- "Remember to say thank you!"
- "You should be proud of..."
- "Aren't you embarrassed about...?"
- "I bet you're excited to be..."
- "Don't be such a 'sad sack'!"

Other statements are more ambiguous, but may still provide guidance regarding culturally expected emotional states:

- "You have a bad attitude."
- "What's wrong with you?"
- "Settle down—this is no big deal."
- "Your positive outlook is just delightful."
- "You're such a Pollyanna!"

As you can see, direct and nearly direct socialization can occur through positive or negative reinforcement. People can be rewarded for their "good" emotional displays (e.g., through compliments) or punished for their "bad" ones (e.g., through criticism).

All the negative sanctions we discussed earlier can be used to encourage conformity to emotion norms, including verbal reprimands, gossip, ostracism, physical violence, and financial pressures. Even a child who throws a "temper tantrum" might be spanked or lose their allowance.

Indirect socialization into emotion norms is also very common. As a child attending Catholic mass at my local church, I remember looking around at all the somber faces and subdued voices. Prayers were uttered with a calm seriousness; hymns were sung in solemn tones. After ceremonies—on the church steps and sidewalk—my parents spoke in upbeat voices with their friends or the parents of my friends. But during mass, the emotional tenor was restrained. Even when parishioners were invited to interact—to shake hands or hug and say "Peace be with you"—I don't recall any laughter or expressions of joy. If I had yelled out "Peace, Doug!" as I waved enthusiastically to my friend a dozen rows away, I was certain I would have been hushed or scolded, even though no one ever explicitly told me so (see also Nelson 1996:386). All

I did was look around and notice that no loud or long-distance greetings were taking place. I indirectly inferred the norms governing my conduct, including my emotional displays.[1]

Similarly, fans who attend a raucous college football game may infer the feeling rules from those around them, such as the announcers, cheerleaders, mascots, and fellow spectators (Zurcher 1982). How excited should fans be? How proud or disgusted with their team? How much respect or animosity should they feel towards the opposing team? How much compassion, fear, or delight should be displayed at a dangerous tackle or an injury? Through their words, actions, and even wardrobe choices, our companions provide informal cues into expected emotional reactions (see also Peterson 2014). Sometimes, there is a sense that little or no emotional reaction is the best. Thus, competitive rowers (Sinden 2010), police officers (Howard, Tuffin, and Stephens 2000), judges (Bergman Blix and Wettergren 2018), educational administrators (Coupland et al. 2008), veterinarians (Ward and McMurray 2016), and other groups may learn that they need to suppress and deny displays of emotion, in order to appear competent and serious.

Direct and indirect socialization can occur via mediated as well as face-to-face interaction. Television shows and movies, books and magazines, video games and music—all can provide explicit instruction or implicit models to follow (Peterson 2006). Every romantic comedy and reality TV show that ends in a wedding proposal does not merely resolve dramatic tension but provides a potential exemplar (or perhaps a cautionary tale) for how to express emotions when a suitor pops the question (Bachen and Illouz 1996; Schweingruber, Anahita, and Berns 2004). Self-help magazine articles that give relationship advice may also propagate emotion norms, such as those governing the expression of anger or love (Clanton 2006).

4) Emotion Norms Vary over Time and from Group to Group

If emotion norms were set by nature or by a god, then we might expect them to be relatively permanent. But, as human creations, understandings regarding "appropriate feelings" often change, within long and short periods of time (Matt and Stearns 2014).

It is easy to imagine the expectations of my subdued childhood parish evolving. With the addition of a new priest and music director, or the demands of a demographically shifting congregation, perhaps the church would move towards a more emotionally joyful and expressive service. Older parishioners might need to be gently re-socialized, by introducing changes gradually or explaining why the new approach was "better." Younger parishioners would grow up thinking this is how the church had always been.

Or, let's return to the realm of sports. Some commentators have noticed a change in the emotional displays of tennis players.[2] Compared to past decades, it has become increasingly acceptable and commonplace for athletes to audibly talk to themselves on the court. Phrases such as "Come on!" and "Let's go!" can regularly be heard after a good or bad shot. Expectations about these expressions of enthusiasm or frustration have evolved. Other rules—such as the norm against yelling angrily at one's opponent—may or may not evolve, but they are still cultural in origin. They seem moral and logical from particular perspectives, but other points of view are possible. (After all, a good argument could be made that a little "trash talking" would enliven tennis matches.) In the National Football League, meanwhile, there have been repeated efforts to institute "anti-celebration" rules to clarify expectations about proper conduct after a successful play. Some behaviors (such as spiking the ball, dancing, performing back flips) can be seen as inflammatory or "unsportsmanlike," especially if gestures are directed at a member of the opposing team. Every time the NFL adjusts the rules about celebration, an argument might be made that the league's emotional–behavioral norms have morphed or evolved.[3]

Or, consider norms about jealousy in romantic relationships. Gordon Clanton (1989, 2006) argued that beliefs about expressing jealousy evolved significantly in the second half of the last century. From around 1945 through the 1960s, articles in popular magazines (especially those aimed at women readers, such as *Redbook*) usually characterized jealousy as "proof of love" for one's partner. Being a little jealous was described as a good thing: it showed that a person valued a relationship. Pathological, obsessive jealousy was frowned upon, but more mundane experiences of the emotion were deemed inevitable and positive—and perhaps something to purposefully prompt in one's partner. Starting around 1970—after the cultural changes of the tumultuous 1960s—magazine articles began to switch to a new understanding of jealousy as an indication of a personality defect. Rather than proof of love, jealousy was now portrayed as a sign of insecurity or an inability to trust. Individuals were encouraged to reduce or eradicate this possessive emotion (through therapy or self-help techniques), since it was thought to damage romantic relationships and constrain friendly interactions between men and women. The old norm that allowed or encouraged minor jealousy declined but did not die out completely, according to Clanton (1989, 2006). Both points of view could still be found in articles published after 1970, and both shaped expectations regarding the experience and display of jealousy, but the new view became predominant.

Thus, emotion norms are not necessarily permanent or stable. Within a culture or subculture, the rules can and do change over time—what we might call *temporal* or *historical variation*. Moreover (and as I've already implied in this chapter), emotion also varies from group to group—what we might call *cross-cultural variation*.

Consider norms about affection between newlyweds. In the US, there is usually an expectation that brides and grooms express their love publicly, through hugs, kisses, hand holding, gift giving, and verbal pronouncements. An insufficient number of these displays—at wedding ceremonies and in the months that follow—might give family and friends cause for concern. In some cultures, however, newlyweds are expected to be much more restrained.

Imagine a society where tradition dictates that a bride moves into her husband's house, to live alongside her husbands' parents and brothers (and brothers' wives). Also, imagine that these family members are concerned (for social and economic reasons) that the household does not break apart—which is something that a young wife, living under the thumb of her mother-in-law, might want to instigate. In such a setting, there may be strong emotion norms against affectionate displays between newlyweds, in order to discourage husbands from giving priority to their marital bond over their larger familial bonds (see Derné 1994; Stockard 2002).

Norms governing grief can also vary from group to group (Lofland 1985). Some cultures may come to view death as a reason to celebrate a loved one's accomplishments or their passage into heaven, whereas others may view it as a pure heartbreak. In a society where half of one's children may die by age five, parents may be expected to spend less time grieving a child than in a society where the rate is fewer than one-in-a-hundred. A high mortality rate may lead children's death to be seen "less as a tragedy than as a predictable and relatively minor misfortune, one to be accepted with equanimity and resignation as an unalterable fact of human existence" (Scheper-Hughes 1992:275). Similarly, the death of a spouse might be expected to have less of an impact among cultures where the continuation of one's ancestral lineage holds far greater importance than any particular family relationship (Stockard 2002).

5) Emotion Norms Can Be Debatable and Conflicting, even within the Same Culture or Setting

Emotion norms might be said to "govern" the way we feel in almost any situation. A belief in the naturalness or goodness of our culture's norms often makes us feel duty-bound to obey and enforce them. Nevertheless, it's important to recognize that the rules are not necessarily ironclad; there can be wiggle room or controversy surrounding their application. Disagreements can arise even between people who have been socialized by the same or similar groups. Differences may stem from ambiguity or imprecision in the norms, as well as from individuals' idiosyncratic personalities, agendas, or exposure to subtly diverse subcultures (see also Kolb 2014a).

For example, a display of gratitude may be expected upon receiving a birthday present. But exactly how much gratitude? And in what format—words, hugs, thank-you letters, or what? There may be no precise formula, and different opinions may arise regarding the manner in which gratitude is expressed. On some occasions, excitement over a gift might substitute for gratitude. Enthusiastic statements such as "Wow—this gift is so cool!" may be taken as "close enough" to gratitude, due to the satisfaction that the gift-giver may derive from the display, and since the gratitude may be implied on the part of the gift-receiver. On the other hand, some sticklers may be adamant that the words "thank you" be stated explicitly and more than once. In my extended family, there has been disagreement regarding whether a thank-you note needs to be handwritten or if an email or text will suffice.

Disagreements do not necessarily indicate that emotion norms are illusory; perhaps the norms are just not dictatorial or clear-cut. Consider an analogy to fashion. Two brothers or sisters may argue about specific clothing choices while still operating within more general cultural expectations. The siblings may disagree whether a particular shirt goes with a particular pair of pants, while sharing many broader expectations regarding nudity (how much skin to cover), gender (what styles boys vs. girls should wear), colors (no silver pants), and patterns (no stripes mixed with polka dots).

In the study by Simon et al. (1992), the researchers found some disagreement among middle-school girls regarding the norm "One should have romantic feelings for only one boy at a time." Some girls maintained relationships with multiple boyfriends, and even bragged about it: As long as the boys are separated geographically and unaware of the two-timing, what's the harm? Other girls, however, disagreed with and criticized this behavior. As the girls grew older, the researchers found that the level of consensus and obedience to the norm of monogamy also tended to grow.

It is even possible for individuals to disagree with themselves about the proper way to feel in a particular situation. When a roommate leaves yet-another mess in the kitchen, is that a good reason to express mild irritation, loud outrage at the injustice, or amusement at the situation's ridiculousness? When a mysterious dent suddenly appears on our car in a parking lot, is it acceptable to swear loudly? Cry? Laugh? As we react and then look back on our reactions, we may not be certain about the appropriateness of our own feelings. We sometimes consider ourselves *fallible*—capable of being mistaken in our initial responses to situations, leading us to entertain conflicting interpretations of our emotions, our selves, and the situations we inhabit (Davis 2012).

Ambivalence is not necessarily a sign of multiple personality disorder or some other personality flaw. Life is complex, and we can view it from many plausible perspectives (Jacobsen 2023a). Moreover, many situations place competing demands on us, requiring us to balance or harmonize conflicting emotion norms. A student who excels on a test may be expected to be thrilled yet sensitive to classmates who scored poorly (Albas and Albas 1988a); doctors and exotic dancers may both need to balance intimacy with a nonchalant business-as-usual demeanor when interacting with their clientele (Emerson 2001; Lerum 2001); a crime victim may be obliged to testify in a calm and "rational" fashion while still communicating the serious pain or trauma they have suffered (Konradi 1999). In short, people who live in modern societies are exposed to a wide array of emotion norms that are sometimes vague and conflicting. Consequently, people may not simply follow the rules; they may consult and creatively *use* emotion norms as they "interpret, evaluate, and justify their own and others' feelings and expressions" (Thoits 2004:365; see also Loseke 2009).

6) Emotion Norms Can Reflect and Perpetuate Inequality

Let's return to the analogy between laws and emotion norms, pushing the comparison one step further—into the realm of politics. Many have noted that the legal system is not necessarily a neutral arbiter of justice. Rather, laws are the outcome of political agendas and struggles, both in their creation and their application. Should women be allowed to vote? Can same-sex partners get married? What penalty (if any) should be given to those possessing marijuana or cocaine?

Laws don't necessarily serve everyone's interests equally. Rather, they can reflect and reinforce relations of power, with dominant groups exerting greater influence over the crafting, enactment, and enforcement of societal rules (McNamee 2024:176–177). The fact that income from wages tends to be taxed at a higher rate than income from investments—a policy which benefits the wealthiest Americans—might be sardonically described as an example of "The Golden Rule": those with the gold make the rules (Rigney 2001:88).

Similarly, it is possible to ask whether emotion norms are simply cultural preferences which vary according to the benign idiosyncrasies of different groups, or whether some seem tailored to the interests of the powerful (Moon 2005). Consider family relationships. Although the influence between parents and children is bidirectional, it seems safe to say that kids usually have much less say about the emotion norms in their families. Of course, children need to learn manners, so that they can control their tempers and act with empathy and politeness towards others. Parents may work hard to "civilize" children, giving them the emotional competence "to manage their bodies so that they may participate acceptably in the social order of both home and wider social arenas" (Mayall 1998:150; Erickson and Cottingham 2014). On the other hand, sometimes parents may enact or enforce emotion norms in a tyrannical and self-serving fashion. "Don't talk back"—that is, don't disrespectfully argue with one's parents—is an emotion norm that could be used to over-dominate or limit democratic input (Gubrium 1992).[4]

The assumption that women are "naturally" more empathetic and nurturing—while seeming to be a compliment or virtue—can also lead to inegalitarian consequences. Wives may operate under feeling rules that require them to be more accessible, sensitive, and supportive than their husbands are, leading to an unequal division of labor at home (Schrock and Knop 2014). The gendered nature of emotion norms may help explain why mothers kiss more scraped knees, wipe more tears, engage in more active listening, and perform other interpersonal work that keeps families close and functional (Deutsch 1999; Erickson and Cottingham 2014).

Emotion norms also generate inequalities outside the home. Consider our places of work.[5] Often the least-paid employees must perform the most strenuous tasks, as when customer service representatives face the brunt of customer dissatisfaction and misbehavior. Mid-and upper-level managers, by comparison, tend to be protected from negative emotions both by *organizational shields* (such as administrative assistants who limit contact with the public) and by *status shields* (the power and prestige that discourages others from "venting" on them). Employers can thus require lower-level employees to abide by emotion norms ("Always smile, and never reciprocate anger to a customer") that accentuate existing inequalities of income and power. Emotion norms can accentuate gender and racial inequality in employment, as well. For example, female workers may be expected to provide more emotional support to their customers, patients, or students than male workers are (Bellas 2001). Black men may not feel as free to express discontent in the workplace, compared to their white male counterparts, due to greater risk of being considered "scary" or "threatening" rather than "passionate" (Wingfield 2010). Meanwhile, professional athletes may be told by fans and employers to keep their thoughts and feelings to themselves, rather than tweet and protest about racial injustice in the criminal justice system (Williams, Bryant, and Carvell 2019).

Emotion norms can even be implicated in the ideologies that justify the class and power inequalities that pervade an entire society. In feudal times, great disparities in wealth were justified by reference to nobles' "birthright" and the "divine right of kings"; slavery, in turn, has been defended via notions of innate inferiority (McNamee 2024). These cognitive belief systems tend to be accompanied by corresponding emotion norms (Loseke 2009). If inequality is warranted, then subordinates should experience calm resignation or perhaps shame at their lowly position, but not hostility or outrage. Currently, many Americans believe that their country is a meritocracy, where one's economic success is primarily the result of talent and hard work. Under this ideology, the successful should take pride in their apparent skills and determination, and the poor should feel embarrassment or remorse for their plight. Downplayed are the many nonmerit factors that influence success—such as being born to wealthy parents, having affordable access to high-quality education and health care, graduating college during a boom rather than a recession, knowing people in high places, and so on (McNamee 2024). The myth of meritocracy may thus condition us to blame ourselves for our economic failures rather than cultivating emotions that may lead us to reform or rebel against existing structural arrangements (Kwate and Meyer 2010; Schwalbe et al. 2000).

Emotional Deviance: How to Violate Emotion Norms

Everybody commits emotional deviance at some point. It's impossible to avoid. On some occasions, we can't help but exhibit feelings that violate our companions' expectations. Perhaps we haven't fully learned the emotion norms yet or were socialized to a different set of guidelines. Perhaps we lack the will or the ability to conform, such as when we are suffering from insomnia or a migraine. Or, in some instances, perhaps the fault lies with cultural expectations that are unrealistic, unfair, or unnecessarily restrictive. We may even choose, consciously, to transgress emotional norms because we believe that they need to be changed. At one point or another, all of us will violate the explicit or implicit rules that govern feelings. In *The Managed Heart*, Hochschild (1983) identified five ways to commit emotional deviance. Let's end this chapter by examining these options, as they can help us appreciate the pervasiveness and significance of emotion norms in society and in our own lives.

The first and most obvious way to deviate from emotion norms is to display the wrong *type* of feeling. Here a person experiences a feeling that simply seems immoral, illogical, or inappropriate: a person feels one particular emotion when they should be feeling something completely different. A young woman, for example, is expected to be very happy when her friends and family throw her a bridal shower. After all, an entire party—complete with food, drinks, gifts, and games—has been assembled in her honor. However, perhaps the stress of the event prompts different emotions (Montemurro 2002). Perhaps the bride does not enjoy being the center of attention for hours; or, perhaps celebrating with an odd collection of acquaintances (e.g., old friends, new friends, mother, mother-in-law, and others) proves uncomfortable. A bride who expresses anger or frustration (rather than gratitude and happiness) could be informally "charged" with experiencing and displaying the wrong type of feeling. Onlookers might judge her harshly.[6]

The second way to commit emotional deviance involves our *intensity*—we can exhibit too much or too little of a particular emotion (Hochschild 1983:64). A feeling might be entirely appropriate, but not in the amount being displayed. Consider wedding proposals. This important event, where one person asks to become a life partner with another, is usually emotionally intense (Bachen and Illouz 1996; Schweingruber et al. 2004). Most people I know would be taken aback by a "ho-hum" attitude. Imagine a lackluster suitor speaking in a lethargic tone: "It occurred to me today that we get along OK. We don't seem to fight too much. I suppose we could try getting married and see if it works out. What do you think?"

Clearly, our emotions can be too strong as well as weak. We can exhibit a surplus of nervousness, anger, fear, or even love. For example, individuals may avoid and criticize classmates who appear excessively nervous about an upcoming exam (Albas and Albas 1988b) or gossip about driving companions who cry in terror when a homeless person approaches the car at a stop light (cf. Esala and Del Rosso 2020). Mothers who decide to homeschool their children may be criticized by friends and relatives for demonstrating "excessive emotional intensity" (Lois 2013). Such women may be accused of feeling overprotective of their children, overly arrogant about their abilities to teach the necessary information, and overly fervent in their religious or moral beliefs.

The third way to violate emotion rules is *duration*—to display a feeling for an inappropriate length of time (Hochschild 1983:64). Thus, it is possible to have the correct feeling, in the right intensity, but to experience it too briefly or too protractedly. For instance, you might expect a friend to feel sad, with moderate intensity, when a pet cat dies. However, if the cat-lover were to wear black and exhibit a somber mood for over a year, then you might think that the mourning has "gone on far too long." Even the loss of a parent, spouse, or child can be met with expectations that the bereaved will achieve "closure" at a pace that some individuals simply cannot match (Berns 2011). On the other hand, a widower might be informally "charged" with mourning for an insufficient length of time, if he were to join www.match.com and begin dating just days after the death of a spouse.

A fourth way to be emotionally deviant is to experience an emotion too early or too late (Hochschild 1983:66). Our feelings can be deemed misfitting if we have what appears to be a "premature" or "delayed" reaction. A person can conform with respect to the type, intensity, and duration, but still violate an emotion norm if their *timing* is off. When a parent dies, for example, it would usually be appropriate for the person to experience grief (type), causing tremendous sadness and tears (intensity), for days, weeks, or even months (duration). However, if someone began grieving because their "mom just turned seventy-five and will likely pass away in the next decade," then most might negatively judge that emotional display as premature. Alternatively, imagine a scenario where a parent passed away but it did not fully impact the child until months or years later—perhaps when the deceased's absence at a wedding became a stark reality. People might expect grief the first six months after a parent dies, but if the feeling does not manifest itself until a later date, then the mourner might be judged emotionally deviant for not seeking and achieving "closure" at the proper time (see also Berns 2011; Goodrum 2008). Similarly, the sympathy that others express to us must be conveyed at the "right" time. Imagine a person writes "Sorry to hear that!" in response to an acquaintance's six-months-old tweet about a stressful day at work. The condolences may be admonished with "Why on earth are you bothering to reply to this now?" (Brownlie and Shaw 2019:114).

Let's consider a lighter example. When I was about ten years old, my mother entered me into a free raffle or lottery at a local store—to receive a huge (six foot tall) Christmas stocking filled with toys. Amazingly, I won the prize. But I had no idea that my mom had entered me in the contest, as she did not want to get my hopes up. When the store manager called to tell me I had won a giant stocking, I was perplexed. "Some man is telling me I won a big sock," I uttered with confusion to my mother and sister, who were nearby. When my mom took the phone and discovered what had happened, she explained the news to me, and I was thrilled. "Cool! Thanks Mom!" I said. But my sister was concerned with my behavior on the phone: "You didn't say 'thanks' or act excited at all," she scolded me. Although I expressed some gratitude to the store manager when we picked up the stocking, in my sister's mind my display was too little (intensity) and too late (timing).

The fifth way to violate emotion norms is through the *placing* of a feeling, when the audience or venue is inappropriate (Hochschild 1983:67). Sometimes we can experience the "correct" emotion at the "right" time (such as excitement immediately upon receiving a prize), but still be emotionally deviant, even if the intensity and duration of our feelings are at acceptable levels.

For example, if a student receives an "A+" on a midterm exam, she may be expected to display excitement, happiness, and/or pride for a short while, right after receiving her grade. However, imagine she is surrounded by two friends who studied just as hard as she did, but who performed more poorly, receiving a "C" and a "D." Those two friends are probably not the best audience for a celebratory display; in fact, they may judge such conduct as insensitive gloating and proceed to "cut her down to size" (Harris 1997:12). Rightly or wrongly, the "A+" student would be deemed emotionally deviant and may receive sanctions from her companions in the form of criticism, gossip, or ostracism (Albas and Albas 1988a).

In addition to excitement and pride, less positive feelings may be out of place as well. For example, many weddings include an invitation for guests to speak up if anyone knows a good reason why the ceremony should not proceed. Most would look unfavorably at a guest who chose to voice negative sentiments about the groom's personality, however valid those concerns may be. Or, consider grief in the classroom. If one of my students were to lose a relative, and was sobbing audibly in class, I might ask him or her to take a brief leave or meet with me individually.[7] Rightly or wrongly, the emotion norms to which I have been socialized lead me to treat strong displays of grief as (usually) improper in the classroom, even if the type, intensity, duration, and timing of the emotion are appropriate (see also Bellas 1999; Meanwell and Kleiner 2014).

Social media, such as Facebook, Twitter, and TikTok, have complicated the notion of placing, since digital platforms involve amorphous and wide-ranging audiences. A *dyadic* interaction involves two people; a *triadic* interaction involves three. Tian and Guo (2021:772) have described social networking sites as forums for *n-adic* interaction because the number of participants is "uncertain, diverse, and invisible." Expressions of grief, love, hatred, amusement, and other feelings may generate unanticipated reactions from a person or group that wasn't imagined when a post was created. This chapter's **Spotlight on Research** further explores what happens when emotion norms go online.

Spotlight on Research

Norms about Mourning on Facebook

An interesting and accessible study of emotion norms was conducted by then-graduate student Jakob Borrits Sabra (2017) in the article " 'I Hate When They Do That!': Netiquette in Mourning and Memorialization Among Danish Facebook Users." Sabra wanted to investigate social expectations regarding the expression of grief online. To do that, he conducted an internet survey with Facebook users, sharing a questionnaire through his personal networks and encouraging his contacts to share it further. Sabra (2017:30) collected demographic and quantitative data from respondents, but his emphasis was on the 166 answers he received to an open-ended question: "What is your opinion on sharing mourning and remembrance on social media?"

Sabra (2017:33) argues that he found evidence for "tacit social rules for grief expressions ... on Facebook." Respondents often had firm views regarding appropriate and inappropriate ways to grieve online. For instance, one respondent said, "If one day you are 'in grief' and express it in a ten line status update and the next day upload a picture of your delicious tuna sandwich, I, personally, find it difficult to take the first [post] seriously" (Sabra 2017:33). This example echoes our discussion of *duration*—the idea that people can violate emotion norms by feeling a "correct" emotion but for a length of time that is deemed too short or too long. In this case, moving too quickly from sadness to lightheartedness was judged harshly, similar to what can happen in face-to-face interaction. *Intensity* was also a factor in Sabra's study. Some respondents suggested that posters should not use Facebook to express very strong feelings of sadness but should limit themselves to milder posts. This was especially true when mourning an expected death resulting from natural causes (e.g., a grandparent losing a slow battle with cancer); respondents seemed to assume that such "normal" deaths should be managed without releasing a flood of feelings online.

While building on Hochschild's (1983) work, Sabra's research also complicates it. In particular, the concept of *placing* becomes a bit more interesting. Recall that placing is a form of emotional deviance that occurs when people are judged to be expressing an emotion in front of the wrong audience—such as celebrating an "A+" in front of a friend who just received a "D" on the same assignment. Sabra's work highlights the fact social media can be a somewhat amorphous locale. Online interactions may occur with an unknown number of people who have diverse backgrounds and wide-ranging connections to the poster, from intimate loved ones to near strangers. Quoting Marwick and Ellison (2012:379), Sabra refers to this situation as *context collapse*: when "individuals representing multiple social contexts (e.g., work, family, high school acquaintances, close friends) are 'collapsed' into the flat category 'friends' or 'contacts' on social media sites."

Context collapse can lead to dilemmas, such as when intense expressions of grief are broadcast to hundreds of "friends," many of whom may be weakly connected to the mourner. Those with weak ties might feel pressured to offer awkward words of condolences, and these words may come across as hollow. Intense grief was thus deemed better conveyed only to close family and friends, who could provide fitting support. Facebook was endorsed as an appropriate forum for sharing modest expressions of sadness alongside basic information such as cause of death or the date and location of wakes. Some respondents also frowned upon mourners posting pictures of the corpse, the coffin, and even the funeral; perhaps these too were seen as "too intense" to share on a public forum.

Intriguingly, Danish respondents also set limits on confident mentions of spiritual matters while mourning. Making assumptions about the afterlife was seen as inappropriate on Facebook. Respondents did not think mourners should speak as if the deceased were still alive, listening or watching over from beyond. Denmark tends to be more secular than many other countries (Zuckerman 2008), including the US, so that may help explain this taboo.

Sabra's research was not intended to be definitive. The sample was not representative of all Facebook users in Denmark, let alone users in other countries. And, even within the study's sample, respondents were not of one mind (see the earlier section in this chapter on norms being "debatable"). Moreover, social media can change rapidly. As platforms offer new methods of interaction and take old ones away, subtle or seismic shifts in expectations about online interaction may occur.

What the study does provide is ample food for thought and some concepts you can test out in your everyday life. What do you think about the "netiquette" that Sabra uncovered among his respondents? Have you encountered similar or different mourning norms on Facebook? Do you think those norms may vary between sites, such as Facebook vs. Twitter? Do you think "context collapse" affects what emotions you express online and how others respond to you? While Sabra focused on grief, you might consider implications for the expression of other kinds of feelings online, such as anger or love.

Exercises

1 Identify at least one emotion norm that shapes the behavior of yourself, your friends, and/or your relatives. Can you explain why a norm that seems "natural" or "logical" is actually cultural? Try to make the argument that another group of people (real or hypothetical) might develop a different set of expectations regarding the emotion norm.
2 Pick a situation—such as a family dinner, a romantic date, a college party, a sporting event, or some other occasion. Describe five ways that a person could be emotionally deviant within the situation, using the concepts of type, intensity, duration, timing, and placing.
3 Consider complicating the examples you used in the first two exercises. Can you explain how an emotion norm you discussed might be learned via direct and indirect socialization; debated between two people or within an individual's mind; or used to maintain power or superiority?

4 Try to answer the questions posed at the end of the Spotlight on Research for this chapter. You might also read for yourself Sabra's (2017) article examining mourning norms on Facebook.

Notes

1 For a more technical and thorough overview of children's socialization into emotions, see Gordon (1989).
2 For example, see http://deadspin.com/why-do-tennis-players-say-come-on-so-much-1249903336 (downloaded October 15, 2013).
3 For example, see: www.nfl.com/news/nfl-relaxing-touchdown-celebration-rules-for-players-0ap3000000810537 (downloaded July 14, 2023).
4 One of my students made an interesting argument in a reflection paper on this section. They argued that emotion norms can also reproduce inequality by exacerbating discrimination against people with mental illness: "For many people, mental illness has an effect on the way they feel or express different emotions and they may become ostracized because of this limited mindset that claims we are supposed to feel the exact same way as our peers in situations that can have multiple impacts on people. There is already a huge stigma surrounding mental health and the idea that we are expected to all feel the same way in response to an event only provides those aligned against mental health and its effects on the diagnosed with more reason to side against them."
5 Chapter 5 of this book (on emotional labor) will discuss these inequalities in greater depth.
6 Esala and Del Rosso (2020) argue that individuals who are anxious about routine activities—such as going to sleep or eating a meal at a restaurant—also tend to be accused of the "violation" of exhibiting the wrong *type* of emotion.
7 I tend to apply these expectations to myself as well. In January of 2013, my father died tragically and unexpectedly, a victim of gun violence. When I began teaching my classes a week later, I was still riddled with shock, grief, and anger. However, I felt pressure to conceal these emotions in the classroom, where I thought they would be too distracting and not "teachable."

Suggested Readings

Hochschild's *The Managed Heart* is a crucial resource for those interested in the sociology of emotions. Its fourth chapter further explains emotion norms and also discusses their role in psychiatrists' diagnosis of problematic feelings.

Hochschild, Arlie Russell. 1983. "Feeling Rules." Chapter 4 in *The Managed Heart*. Berkeley, CA: University of California Press.

Christina Kotchemidova provides a compelling example of an historical approach to emotions, tracing the ascendance of the norm of "cheerfulness" over a period of three centuries.

Kotchemidova, Christina. 2005. "From Good Cheer to 'Drive-by Smiling': A Social History of Cheerfulness." *Journal of Social History* 39(1):5–37. https://doi.org/10.1353/jsh.2005.0108.

For a succinct cross-cultural comparison of understandings and norms about love, you might read the work of Steve Derné. The author also considers the sociological factors that shape *why* cultural variability exists.

Derné, Steve. 1994. "Structural Realities, Persistent Dilemmas, and the Construction of Emotional Paradigms: Love in Three Cultures." Pp. 281–308 in *Social Perspectives on Emotion*, edited by William M. Wentworth and John Ryan. Greenwich, CT: JAI.

Donileen Loseke (2009) extends the concept of emotion norms in her article examining the first four nationally televised speeches that President Bush made after the attacks on September 11, 2001. Bush invoked and affirmed "emotion codes"—widespread (but by no means universally accepted) cultural understandings regarding what to feel and how to express it. The chapter by Loseke and Kusenbach (2008) gives more background to the notion of emotion codes and addresses other ideas that are central to the sociology of emotions.

Loseke, Donileen R. 2009. "Examining Emotion as Discourse: Emotion Codes and Presidential Speeches Justifying War." *Sociological Quarterly* 50:497–524. https://doi.org/10.1111/j.1533-8525.2009.01150.x

Loseke, Donileen R. and Margarethe Kusenbach. 2008. "The Social Construction of Emotion." Pp. 511–529 in *Handbook of Constructionist Research*, edited by Jaber F. Gubrium and James A. Holstein. New York: Guilford.

Daniel Rigney provides a helpful introduction to the concept of social norms by highlighting its metaphorical connotations. Our companions can act as proverbial police officers, judges, jurors, and executioners when we break the implicit laws of social interaction.

Rigney, Daniel. 2001. "Society as Legal Order." Chapter 5 in *The Metaphorical Society: An Invitation to Social Theory*. Lanham, MD: Rowman & Littlefield.

3 Emotion Management

In the previous chapter, we discussed emotion norms, the cultural expectations that govern the feelings we experience and display. These formal and (usually) informal rules tell us what emotions should be felt or expressed in particular situations. Our companions socialize us into these norms, by providing explicit instructions and implicit models to follow. The rules pervade our lives, and require us to try to "fit in."

Chapter 2 thus begs some questions: How do we navigate these emotion norms? What do we do when our emotions don't match others' expectations? How do we avoid—most of the time—violating these pervasive and intricate rules?

In Chapter 3, we will examine the interactional strategies people use to control emotions. People put great effort into shaping their emotional experiences and displays—efforts that are often but not always successful. Like actors on a stage (Goffman 1959), human beings can perform or manage their emotions, thereby manipulating what audiences see and think. We can "put on a show" by feigning gratitude or faking confidence. Or, like method actors (Hochschild 1983:38) we can try to immerse ourselves into a role, and work ourselves into a desired emotional state, so that we actually become grateful or confident.[1]

Surface Acting

The simplest way that people can control their feelings is by putting on a proverbial mask. We can attempt to display an emotion that we are not actually feeling. Human beings can purposefully hide, disguise, or exaggerate feelings. Sociologists call this *surface acting*—which could be defined as *managing how one appears to feel* (Hochschild 1983:37).

The concept of surface acting can help us recognize a wide range of techniques that we have to control what others perceive about our emotions. Let's imagine that you receive a gift (perhaps for your birthday) that you deem atrocious; maybe it's a sweater from your grandmother that you will never wear. You could say something honest—such as "Wow, this is a terrible gift, Grandma. Don't expect me to send you a 'thank you' note for this one!"—but

DOI: 10.4324/b23334-3

that would be cruel and would likely violate your family's expectations. To protect your grandmother's feelings, and to escape the kinds of sanctions that your family might impose upon such a flagrant violation of emotion norms, you can pretend to feel excited and grateful about the sweater. Through a variety of tactics, you can act as if you like it more than you do. For the sake of clarity, let's itemize five of them, using the example of the sweater and drawing parallels with research by emotions scholars.

Five Surface Acting Strategies

1) Wording

Human beings can select their words carefully in order to give the impression that they are feeling something that they are not. Thus, rather than saying something frank but cruel about your grandmother's present ("This is terrible!"), you could choose to be less candid but nicer ("Cool—thanks! Good color!"). And, even though you don't envision ever wearing the sweater in public, you might proclaim "I love it! I can use this for both school and work, which is fantastic!"

Similarly, teachers may disguise the feelings of boredom, irritation, or even anger that students can sometimes elicit. Many instructors seek to model the emotional tenor of civil inquiry and debate, while making class entertaining (Bellas 1999; Roberts and Smith 2002). Thus, a student's potentially offensive remark might be met with "That raises a good topic" as the instructor masks a negative reaction with a calmer, more positive demeanor. Or, a teacher may start class by saying "We're covering an interesting topic today!" even though they might (on at least some occasions) be tempted to say "I've taught today's material too many times and am utterly bored by it."

2) Tone of Voice

If you were to express your true feelings about an undesirable gift, you might use a negative tone of voice that conveyed your actual disinterest, disappointment, or frustration. Even the word "Thanks" can be uttered in a way that drips with sarcasm. Instead of doing that, you might surface act by adopting a positive tone of voice that feigned enthusiasm and appreciation. Imagine a "Thank you!" that is spoken loudly, in a higher pitch, compared to a quietly sighed "Thanks I guess" that sounds bored or annoyed.

Similarly, but in a much different context, 9-1-1 call takers need to monitor their tone of voice carefully, so as to quickly ameliorate rather than inflame potentially volatile situations. Tracy and Tracy (1998) examined the 9-1-1 training manuals of the police department of a western city, and found guidelines such as:

- Do not show any personal feelings, either friendly or unfriendly. Watch your tone of voice. Try to talk in an even, steady pace.

- Do not let your tone of voice sound bored or uncaring. ...Display an interest in the caller.
- Do not belittle callers for not having a proper understanding of what ... constitutes an "emergency." (Adapted from Tracy and Tracy 1998:400)

Given these instructions, call takers could be expected to engage in a large amount of surface acting via tone of voice—especially because the sound of their voice is all a caller has access to. A call taker might be bored, irritated, or upset by a particular caller. However, to conform to the organization's rules, the worker might mask those feelings by adopting a tone that seems neutral yet concerned. If so, that would be a relatively clear case of surface acting.

3) Facial Expressions

People listen closely to our words and the sound of our voice; they can also monitor our emotional displays by scrutinizing our facial expressions. To return to our original example: It's possible that one's grandmother might notice that the sweater she gave you prompted a frown of annoyance or a blank look of boredom. Either reaction on your part might be interpreted as hurtful and emotionally deviant. Given those options, you may choose to force a smile—and not just a closed-lip grin but a generous display of teeth. You might even open your eyes and mouth wide as you say "Wooowww, great sweater Grandma!" Certainly, you would want to avoid looking upwards and rolling your eyes, which is a conventional symbol of sarcasm.

A different but parallel example can easily be found in the realm of gambling. Anyone who has played a few hands of poker might be able to testify to the discipline it takes to bluff—to make a large bet on a weak hand, while appearing confident or nonchalant. One's companions may closely examine your face, among other indicators, for any "tells." More accomplished gamblers might let themselves be caught committing a bluff on purpose, and even portray a (manufactured) look of frustration, in order to accomplish a larger and more consequential bluff on a subsequent occasion (Zurcher 1970).

Human beings may be more or less skillful at manipulating facial expressions, but it is a tactic that nearly everyone can at least attempt, when interacting with friends, family, co-workers, and strangers. Medical students must learn to hide any looks of nervousness, disgust, or sexual attraction as they begin to interact with cadavers and patients (Smith and Kleinman 1989). To put on a show for a jury, defense attorneys may strategically maintain a neutral, distracted, or bored expression on their face as the prosecution presents incriminating evidence about their client (Flower 2018). Bouncers and border patrol agents may maintain firm and stoic expressions, to hide fear and minimize resistance as they control others' movements (Rivera 2015; Ward and McMurray 2016).

The Covid-19 pandemic was difficult for many reasons. One challenge was that wearing face masks limited our use of facial expressions to show others what we are feeling. While the eyes remain visible, a mask obscures the mouth, thus making it difficult to spontaneously or strategically express certain emotions (Nester, Fischer, and Arnold 2020). The bottom half of the face is crucial when displaying a big or small smile (teeth or no teeth), a pout or a frown, a wide-open look of surprise, or a curled-lip expression of disgust. It was disconcerting to lose that communication strategy, both as speakers and listeners, which shows how much we take for granted the subtle cues we use to present and discern apparent feelings.

4) Bodily Gestures

Further below the face, we have other bodily tools useful for managing emotional displays. For example, if you were to display your feelings in a blunt manner, then you might drop an undesirable sweater with a shrug of disinterest, as if to say "Boring present, Grandma. Not something I will use." Instead, to avoid appearing mean-spirited and ungrateful, you could choose to surface act to give the opposite impression. You might use your arms to lift the sweater up high for everyone in the room to see, and then hold it against your chest as you discussed its "soft fabric" or "perfect size." You might even walk quickly across the room to give your grandmother an enthusiastic hug.

A related example, though in a strikingly different setting, can be found in Martin's (2005) research on rape workers. Police officers, prosecutors, doctors, nurses, victim advocates, and other personnel use a variety of emotion management strategies as they deal with victims of sexual assault. Workers may purposefully craft an image of true care and concern, even though they may be experiencing a different emotion or a mixture of emotions—such as discomfort, disdain, frustration, anger, and/or sadness. One deputy sheriff explained his surface acting in this manner:

> I like to get lower than the victim. If she stands, I sit; if she sits, I lay on the floor. I hold her hand and she won't let mine go, even while I'm driving. One time, a girl was raped on the beach and her mother and her sat in the back seat [of the patrol car] and she held my hand over my shoulder while I drove the car. ... She trusted me so completely. She told me every little thing. It was wonderful for her... and for us [for the investigation].
>
> (Martin 2005:209)

Here, the deputy can be seen as using bodily gestures in an attempt to convey sympathy and support—and perhaps a sense of being "with" and "for" rather than "above" and "apart from" the victim—as he sought information helpful for obtaining a conviction.

5) Clothing

On some occasions, even the clothes we wear can convey what we are feeling to our companions. To convey gratitude to your grandmother for her gift, you could adjust your wardrobe strategically. For example, you might "try on" the sweater in her presence, and then continue to wear it for as long as the family gathering lasts. Or, if you put some extra thought into convincing your grandmother that you "truly" do like and appreciate her gift, then you might remember to wear the sweater the next time you see her—perhaps two months later at a different family gathering. Here your choice of clothing would qualify as surface acting, since you are managing how you appear to feel: you are trying to portray gratitude and enthusiasm through your wardrobe choices.

Similarly, a person who wants to appear relaxed and jovial might don khaki shorts and a bright Hawaiian "party" shirt. Such an outfit would be inappropriate while interviewing at a law firm, where formal attire would likely be chosen to convey one's respect and serious demeanor. When in mourning, Americans often wear black to display their grief; on the other hand, black lingerie might express lustful feelings to one's romantic partner. Connections between emotion and color vary within and across cultures (Fine et al. 1998). In many countries (such as China, India, and Japan), the clothing most associated with mourning has been white, not black (Taylor 2009:209).

Arguably, a doctor's white lab coat (or scrubs) conveys a certain emotional tenor—seriousness, depersonalization, and scientific rationality (Emerson 2001). The outfit contrasts nicely with that of a "badass"—an adolescent whose leather jacket, metal spikes, and boots seem strategically chosen to convey a tough, mean, and aggressive demeanor (Katz 1988). Perhaps a more straightforward example can be found at the restaurant chain Texas Roadhouse,[2] where staff can be seen wearing shirts that proclaim "I [heart] my job!" There a wardrobe choice—most likely dictated by the employer—is intended to convey a particular emotion (love) to an audience of customers, regardless of what an employee happens to feel at any given moment.

This list of surface acting strategies is not exhaustive. People may surround themselves with physical objects (such as posters, photographs, buttons, or trophies) in order to convey love, pride, or some other feeling; a politician who wears a flag pin comes to mind. A carefully selected tattoo (temporary or permanent) may serve the same purpose, as could hair or makeup. People are creative and may invent or adopt a range of mundane surface acting strategies—including in the digital world, where many an acronym and emoticon has been deployed (Derks, Fischer, and Bos 2008). Lol ;-). One's account on Instagram can be carefully stocked with images designed to give the impression that a person is successful, fun-loving, and consistently happy. Or, after a tragedy, individuals may post online "pictures of a program from a victim's funeral, a treasured photo of one of the victims, or a close-up of the items at a memorial" in order to give the impression (accurate or not) that they are in mourning (Pearce 2020:312).

Nevertheless, this five-part list makes the general point: the emotions that human beings express are not simply natural, inevitable, or automatic. Rather, people can "work" on the feelings they display. By strategically selecting their words, tone of voice, facial expressions, bodily gestures, and clothing, human beings can "fake" or at least alter their emotional displays. We can present an outward demeanor that exaggerates the gratitude we feel for a gift, hides the nervousness we experience at a job interview, or disguises the frustration of waiting in a long line at a store.

Deep Acting

Emotion management does not stop at the surface level. Human beings can also *deep act*, by *managing how they actually feel* (Hochschild 1983:42). Sometimes people don't just want to appear less nervous, they want to actually *be* less nervous. On some occasions, we may want to make ourselves actually feel (and not merely feign) more gratitude or less frustration. Deep acting can be done to shape the impressions we make on others—for example, to show them that we are not emotionally deviant. Alternatively, deep acting may be done for our own benefit, as we pursue an emotional state that seems more desirable.

Three Deep Acting Techniques

There are at least three different types of deep-acting strategies people can use to modify their emotions. The last category—cognitive deep acting—is the most interesting, probably the most widely used, and has been most thoroughly researched by sociologists. By using these techniques, we can try to evoke a feeling that is weak or absent, suppress an unwanted feeling, or transform an emotional state into a different experience entirely (Hochschild 1979).

1) Bodily Deep Acting

One way to try to change the way you feel is by focusing on your body—more specifically, your level of physical arousal (e.g., getting "worked up" or "calmed down"). For example, anger or frustration can sometimes make us feel like our blood is "boiling." We may clench our fists and press our teeth together as if containing a burst negativity that wants to get out. To reduce this feeling, individuals might purposefully work on their bodies in a number of ways. They may take a slow, deep breath, unclench their fists, and count to ten before saying or doing anything that might come across as rude.

Parallel examples can be found in many realms of social life. In a study by Albas and Albas (1988a/b), some college students reported taking baths in order to calm nerves over exams. Chewing on pens, jiggling a leg, and other strategies were also used to dispel nervous energy. Studies of self-injury—cutting, burning, bruising, and the like—have found that such practices may also be pursued in an attempt to manage emotions (Adler and Adler 2011; Chandler 2012). Interviewees have suggested that they self-injure in order to feel a sense of control, to find relief or escape from negative emotions, and to overcome "numbness." In a related (but less severe) example, a flight attendant in Hochschild's (1983:113) study said that she dealt with unruly customers in a bodily fashion: "I chew on ice, just crush my anger away." Meanwhile, some yoga advocates believe that the physical postures they perform will help release pent-up feelings (Johnston 2021:587).

Bodily emotion work may be done to become either amped up or calmed down. Often, there can be a fine line, or perhaps a tenuous middle ground, between being too excited and too relaxed. Athletes and students both report seeking an optimum level of arousal—a state somewhere in between being too nervous or excited and being too calm or comfortable (Albas and Albas 1988b; Peterson 2014). Being excessively worked up (or "jittery") might interfere with one's performance on an exam or in the field, as much as being overly relaxed (or disengaged, sloppy). Ritualistic behaviors on the sports field—which are sometimes dismissed as superstition—can be efforts to maintain a balance between being alert and being at ease. For example, tennis players may hop up and down, and then shake their heads back and forth, in order to prepare to receive a serve from a hard-hitting opponent. Or, consider the sorts of routines that baseball players engage in:

> When I ... get into the [batter's] box ... I go through a little ritual—pull my batting gloves up, tighten them a little bit, hit my cleats with the bat. I always keep the bat in my left hand. I step in with my back foot first, get it comfortable, hit my helmet three times, come up with the bat and take a relaxing swing.
>
> (Snyder and Ammons 1993:127)

These sorts of actions can be interpreted as bodily deep acting, if the goal is to shape one's emotions—calibrating just the right mix of nervousness, confidence, and concentration—by manipulating one's body. Similarly, students adjust their intake of food,[3] caffeine, tobacco, and other substances, in an effort to calm nerves or increase alertness, as they prepare for and take exams (Albas and Albas 1988b).

2) Expressive Deep Acting

A second technique for modifying feelings—expressive deep acting—is related to but distinguishable from bodily deep acting. The goal of this strategy is to change an emotional display so that inner feelings might start to match our external appearances (Hochschild 1979:562). For example, when people feel "down," they might choose to act happy in order to improve their mood. The next time you feel a bit gloomy or low, test out this technique: force a smile on your face, look upwards rather than at your feet, put a spring in your step, and check to see whether you feel any better. Sometimes "such playacting can generate internal sensations associated with the displayed state" (Thoits 1985:235). Expressive deep acting can also be used to assuage nervousness.

In Albas and Albas's (1988b) research, a small minority of students dressed formally for exams, in order to look (and thereby feel) more professional and confident. Most other students, however, tended to dress down during exams. A relaxed appearance may also be a form of expressive deep acting, if the goal is (at least partly) to calm nerves by diminishing the "foreboding formality of the examination event and render[ing] it a more everyday, almost homely affair" (Albas and Albas 1988b:265).

Interestingly, the phrase "Fake it until you make it" can be given an emotional spin and linked to expressive deep acting. In her book *On People Management*, the founder of Mary Kay cosmetics invokes that expression as she advises managers to model enthusiasm for workers: On days you don't feel like going to work, managers should try to "act enthusiastic and you will become enthusiastic" (Ash 1984:61).

Unlikely as it may seem, expressive deep acting can also be used to generate negative emotions, rather than suppress or transform them. An athlete may replace a smile with a scowl, in hopes that feelings of jovial camaraderie can be turned into anxiety and aggression—a strategy reminiscent of the expression "putting on your game face" (cf. Gallmeier 1987). Or, sometimes people may try to force themselves to cry in order to make themselves feel sad. This tactic might be used when positive feelings are deemed inappropriate (e.g., at a funeral for a distant relative), when a person wants to begin a grieving process (rather than have it delayed or prolonged), or when an individual wants to fully participate in a solo or group therapy session (e.g., see Thoits 1996).

The concept of expressive deep acting confuses some students, for two reasons. First, it sounds similar to bodily deep acting. The difference is subtle, but it can be stated fairly clearly. Instead of simply changing your physical arousal (like bodily deep acting), expressive deep acting involves a more specific effort to outwardly portray a particular emotional state in order to create it on the inside.

A second confusion arises due to a complicated overlap with surface acting. Remember: surface acting occurs when we manage how we appear to feel to others—for example, by forcing a smile even though we are displeased. The purpose of surface acting is to manage what others see and think about our emotions. If your goal is to manage how you actually feel (by using outward displays to affect your inner feelings), then that is expressive deep acting.[4] In short, surface acting can become deep acting if one's goal switches from feigning a feeling to making a feeling.

3) Cognitive Deep Acting

The most interesting way that people try to modify their emotions is through cognitive deep acting. This strategy occurs when people change their perspective on a situation in order to feel differently about it. When we want to feel differently than we currently do, we can "work on" or manipulate the thoughts, ideas, and images that run through our minds.

For example, after receiving a bad grade on an exam, some students might feel disappointed, sad, or even ashamed. In order to reduce those negative feelings or evoke positive ones, they might try turning their minds toward different sorts of thoughts. To minimize the seriousness of the low score, some students may "justify" (Scott and Lyman 1968) the grade, telling themselves that the situation is not that bad: *A "C" is no big deal— it's just one exam out of the hundreds I'll take in college. This class doesn't matter—it's not part of my major. Five years after I graduate, no one will care what my GPA in college was.* On the other hand, some students might "excuse" (Scott and Lyman 1968) their performance, attributing it to factors out of their control: *I took some unlucky guesses. I was sick the day of the exam, so it's not really my fault that I scored so low. If I wasn't so busy with work, I'm sure I would have aced this exam.*

Similarly, members of 4-H may feel remorse and sadness when the animals they raise are sent to be slaughtered.[5] To manage those negative emotions, they may tell themselves "God gave us animals for food" (Ellis and Irvine 2010:30). Terms such as "livestock" and "market animal" can be used while cute names ("Cupcake," "Jesse") are purposefully avoided, in order to objectify the animal, restrain empathy, and make slaughter seem like destiny. Thus, cognitive deep acting can be employed to manage the emotional struggle of raising and caring for animals that are put to harsh instrumental uses (Ellis and Irvine 2010:31).

Consider a judge overseeing a trial of a man charged with child abuse or murder. She might be tempted to shake her head or curl her lip in disgust, as evidence and motions are presented. In order to suppress that emotion and maintain the impression of neutrality, the judge may remind herself that, in court, everyone must be treated as innocent until proven guilty, that people are sometimes wrongly accused, and that displaying strong emotional reactions could damage her professional reputation (Bergman Blix and Wettergren 2018:143). Or, imagine being a financial advisor who helps clients plan for retirement. As a new or mid-career advisor, your own savings might seem very meager compared to your wealthiest clients who have amassed millions of dollars. The temptation may be to feel envious of your clients and embarrassed by your own net worth. Repeating the mantra *Money does not buy happiness* would be a cognitive deep acting strategy in that situation (Delaney 2012:124–125). You might also purposefully recall meetings with clients who were both extremely wealthy *and* extremely unhappy, to convince yourself that having a smaller bank account is not so bad. Moreover, you might focus your mind on those clients who inherited their money, to make yourself feel prouder of the hard-earned funds you had accumulated. Lastly, you might choose to think about the huge number of people living in poverty in the US, and the billions more around the world, as a way to feel more satisfied with your very comfortable standard of living.

Most financial advisors would probably not choose to avoid wealthy clients, as a way to suppress envy or dissatisfaction. However, there are many occasions when people do try to limit who or what enters their consciousness.

A student who wants to remain calm before an exam may keep away from panicky classmates (Albas and Albas 1988b). Some individuals may organize friendly outings that do not involve sports or dancing, to evade embarrassing reminders of their lack of coordination and rhythm (Harris 1997). A pitcher may steer clear of almost any conversations, to maintain focus during and even preceding a game (Snyder and Ammons 1993). A medical student may try to delay or pass off a sensitive procedure, if it makes them uncomfortable (Smith and Kleinman 1989). People who experience fear, helplessness, or guilt over a social problem (e.g., climate change, racism in their community) might choose to shun any news on that topic (Norgaard 2006). And clearly, individuals may immerse themselves in TikTok videos or epic marathons of television viewing, to avoid thinking about a failed romance or a death in the family.

As my examples have implied, cognitive deep acting is frequently used to try to suppress negative emotions and create positive ones. However, people can also purposefully try to create negative feelings (or a mixture of negative and positive). For example, bill collectors may try to feel angrier at debtors by labeling them "loafers" and "cheats" and not taking seriously their tales of health trouble or unemployment (Hochschild 1983:143). Medical students may occasionally focus on and exaggerate faults in patients' character or behavior, as a way to transform feelings of awkwardness into anger and a sense of superiority (Smith and Kleinman 1989:63). Police officers may (in private conversations) ridicule citizens, as a way of turning frustration over the public's behavior into anger, as well as amusement and moral superiority (Pogrebin and Poole 2003:86).

Or, let's return to sporting events and funerals. In both situations, people may attempt to replace relatively "good" feelings with relatively "bad" ones. Athletes may tell themselves many things in order to evoke agitation and aggression: *Come on, wake up! This is important! You've got to beat that jerk! Don't be a loser!* (A tennis friend of mine called this strategy "Unleashing your inner a**hole.") Similarly, funeral goers may notice that they are deviating from the emotional tenor of the event. In order to conform to social expectations, and to convey the high regard that they actually have for the deceased, an individual might try to evoke sadness by focusing on death and loss: *I'll never ever get see my grandfather again, and he was such a sweet man! I was hoping he would attend my college graduation!* These sorts of thoughts might generate the desired feeling and appropriate display, compared to letting one's mind wander: *That piano player is really good. I wonder what kinds of food will be at the reception.*

The concepts of bodily, expressive, and cognitive deep acting should not be reified or taken too seriously. They are simply three terms that are useful for thinking about the strategies people use to manage their feelings. To be sure, there may be other strategies that might escape or extend this list. If meditation and hypnosis can be emotion management (Thoits 1990), as well as laughter (Francis 1994), bathing, eating, and sleeping (Albas and Albas 1988b), and gambling (Ricketts and Macaskill 2003), then it's clear that virtually any human behavior can be conceptualized as deep acting, as long as a person's intention is (in part) to modify feelings. In addition, it's important to recognize that any given behavior might fit more than one deep acting category. For example, some people listen to music in order to feel calmer, happier, or more excited, or even to wallow in sadness (Schwarz 2018; Wells 1990). That tactic may be as much cognitive (changing one's frame of mind via the lyrics and the distraction from other concerns) as it is bodily (changing one's level of physical arousal via the tempo).

Despite such complexities, these three categories—bodily, expressive, and cognitive deep acting—help us recognize another major social dimension of human emotion. Human beings can, and regularly do, attempt to manage the emotions they experience. With varying degrees of success, people can manipulate their feelings in order to conform to emotion norms and accomplish other goals they set for themselves.

Interpersonal Emotion Management

So far, my discussion has focused on surface and deep acting primarily at an individual level. My examples have centered on lone individuals modifying their own emotional experiences and displays. It is important to recognize, though, that emotion management can be interpersonal—a joint, interactive project. Two or more people can work on emotions, in a collaborative or adversarial manner (Lois 2013:114). The feelings people experience and display can be a group project, assembled with varying degrees of consensus and good will.

Cognitive deep acting—modifying feelings by changing one's thoughts or perspective—can easily be connected to interpersonal emotion management. Arguably, human beings are constantly trying to shape each other's feelings by encouraging some thoughts over others. Friends sometimes make reassuring statements like "There are plenty of fish in the sea" (after a painful breakup) or "I'm sure something even better will come along" (after a missed job opportunity) in an attempt to collaboratively bolster our spirits (Harris 1997). Flight attendants want to make passengers feel relaxed, safe, and welcome (Hochschild 1983); thus, pre-flight safety demonstrations explain what to do "in the unlikely event of a water landing" rather than "if we crash horribly into the ocean." Compare that to rafting guides, who give river rapids ominous names ("Hell's Half Mile," "Satan's Gut!") in order to elicit excitement and a mild amount of fear in customers (Holyfield and Jonas 2003). Or, consider veterinarians who euthanize sick and elderly animals. Once pet owners have made the difficult decision to end a companion animal's life, veterinarians try to assuage the guilt owners may feel: "You did the right thing. … Many people make the mistake of waiting too late … and the animal suffers. It is obvious that you love [your pet] and didn't want him to suffer" (Morris 2012:348).

Bodily deep acting can also be accomplished interpersonally and collaboratively. When I was an undergraduate living in the dorms at UC San Diego,

I participated in a fun tradition. At 10p.m. every night during finals week, students blasted music out of their windows while screaming at the top of their lungs, for around ten minutes. The collective goal was to "release tension" and thereby reduce stress. Similarly, co-workers or friends may invite each other to the gym, to "vent" negative emotions by taking a class in kick boxing or some other form of exercise. Or, consider serious athletes: Football and hockey players frequently bang their helmets together and pound on each other's shoulder pads before a game (Gallmeier 1987; Zurcher 1982), in order to increase feelings of excitement and aggression. All of these actions exemplify a collaborative form of bodily deep acting, since two or more people are attempting to modify feelings by altering at least one person's level of physical arousal.

Collaborative emotion management can occur through surface acting, too. Whenever a parent gives a gentle reminder to express gratitude—as in "What do you say?"—they are encouraging their children to develop manners and spontaneously modify their emotional displays. (If parents wanted their children to work up actual feelings of gratitude, then that would be deep acting—which is also a possibility but might require more careful coaching.) Surface acting can be rehearsed as well as impromptu. Before hosting a dinner party, two spouses may decide not to discuss certain "serious" topics with guests; in so doing, they may collude to display a lighthearted attitude (even if it is not felt).

These examples of interpersonal emotion management are relatively sanguine. Less happily, there are certainly occasions when two or more people work on emotions in a more adversarial rather than cooperative fashion. People can attempt to manage our emotions in ways that fit their own interests more than ours.

For example, sometimes our companions can try to "tear us down" rather than "build us up," even if we wish they wouldn't. When fraternity or sorority members discuss their full social life, their companions who are not in the Greek system might be tempted to say "I don't have to pay for my friends" as a way to deflate any pride or cockiness (Harris 1997:8). Or, successful athletes may find that their friends no longer listen, smile, and nod when they discuss their accomplishments. Our companions may avoid conversational topics or activities that they feel infuse us with "too much" pride or delight—a strategy that can be linked to the expression "I won't give him [or her] the satisfaction."

Interpersonal emotion management can be adversarial when we manipulate others' feelings (against their will) to get what we want. For example, bill collectors may try to make people fearful and embarrassed about overdue payments, despite any objections or counterarguments that the debtors may raise (Hochschild 1983:144). Similarly, detectives may seek compliance from a suspect or witness by manipulating anxiety through "good cop, bad cop" strategies (Rafaeli and Sutton 1991). Fast food restaurants may closely supervise employees, in an effort to suppress any profit-sapping emotions that workers (if left to their own devices) might want to display (Leidner 1999). Con artists, in turn, may attempt to discourage victims from seeking revenge or contacting the police, by saying things that "cool the mark out" (Goffman 1952).

Let's consider a final point, before we close this section. It's important to recognize that emotion management can be—in a loose sense—"interpersonal" even when we seem to be acting alone. Other people can be present in our minds despite being physically absent. For instance, when feeling down, people may remember encouraging words that others have been spoken to them and use those comments to improve their mood. Or, more adversarially, we may repeatedly recall a mean-spirited remark someone inflicted upon us, allowing the criticism to affect our mood even though we wish it wouldn't. See the **Spotlight on Research** here and in Chapter 5, for more examples of this phenomenon.

Spotlight on Research

Prayer as Emotion Management

Shane Sharp (2010) conducted a fascinating study on "How Does Prayer Help Manage Emotions?" To answer this question, Sharp interviewed sixty-two current and former victims of intimate partner violence from a wide range of religious, socioeconomic, ethnic, racial, and geographical backgrounds. The vast majority of participants had suffered both physical abuse (e.g., being hit, slapped, or kicked) and psychological abuse (e.g., being called "worthless" and threatened with bodily harm). Some were subjected to isolation tactics or to sexual abuse. Sharp asked his respondents questions such as "Did you talk to God during your abusive experiences?" and "How exactly did you find it helpful?"

The author took an agnostic stance in his data collection. He referred to prayer as an *imagined interaction* but defined that term to mean interaction that could not be observed by a third party. He did not take a stand on whether a deity was actually listening or responding.

Sharp found that prayer served as a valuable emotion management resource for these women. About one-third (37 percent) reported that prayer provided another way to express negative emotion—a supportive ear to vent about the anger that abuse generated. Approximately one-quarter (24 percent) said prayer helped maintain their self-esteem by providing positive reflective appraisals. If God is conceived as loving and benevolent, then interacting with such a being may bolster one's self-worth (e.g., "You are special in my eyes"). Prayer can also assuage fears. Approximately one-fifth (21 percent) of respondents suggested that talking to God made them feel safer—either under his protection in this life or by being invited into his presence in the afterlife. The meditative aspects of prayer also helped abused women manage their emotions. Sixteen percent of respondents said that prayer helped them "zone out" or reduce the level of attention they gave to negative stimuli, such as derogatory and threatening language. Lastly, thirteen percent of the women indicated that prayer helped manage emotions by fostering forgiveness. If God is conceived as a compassionate and loving parent who can forgive anything, then an imagined interaction with him may encourage a similar mindset and provide a model for how to let go of anger and bitterness.

Both the religious and irreligious might find Sharp's argument convincing: Human beings can use prayer to manage their emotions, regardless of whether any particular deity is "really" listening or speaking to them.

If you accept this finding, then you might consider two extrapolations from it. First, people might also manage their emotions by imagining others who are not deities. For example, when we are feeling down we can imagine encouraging words that a friend or family member might say if they were with us. Second, we can ask whether the "other" needs to be so benevolent. On some occasions, people may try to overcome lethargy by imagining harsh comments from a coach, parent, or vengeful deity.

So, regardless of whether you are religious, can you recall a time when you used an imagined interaction to manage your emotions?

Is Emotion Management Dishonest?

When I teach the concepts of surface and deep acting, my students sometimes ask me whether anyone who manages their emotions is a "liar." Isn't it dishonest to pretend to have a feeling through surface acting? Isn't it also somewhat "phony" to conjure up an emotion via deep acting?

There are situations in which surface and deep acting are fundamentally dishonest. A student might successfully fool a teacher with faux despair over a (non-existent) crashed computer, in order to obtain an extension—just as a con artist might portray utter certainty while selling someone a worthless product or sham investment. In either case, surface or deep acting may be employed. The con artist and the student may simply put on a mask of assuredness or distress, or they may talk themselves into those emotions (temporarily) via cognitive deep acting. With surface acting, the lie is simple: trick the audience into believing a falsehood. With deep acting, the lie is compound: trick yourself into believing something false, so that you can successfully portray a falsehood to an audience.

On the other hand, there are many occasions where surface and deep acting seem relatively honest. For example, suppose the student's computer really did self-destruct at the worst possible moment, in an upsetting way. In that context, it might make sense for a student to pause outside a professor's office and work up the necessary distress through cognitive deep acting—perhaps by thinking "I need a good grade in this course! It totally sucks that my computer died, and it's not my fault!" Or, the student may focus only on their exterior display, and stick to surface acting. Either way, the degree of dishonesty may be minimal. The student's goal may be to make the instructor understand how terrible and unavoidable the predicament *really* is. If the student's distress were only expressed in the privacy of a dorm room, and not displayed in office hours, then the professor may remain blind to the "real truth" of the situation. Thus, a student may choose to strategically re-experience and re-enact the distress, in order to convince a professor of something real rather than something false. This is a far cry from the blatantly dishonest student who simply fabricates a made-up excuse in order to cover for procrastination or excessive alcohol consumption.

Moreover, even flagrantly dishonest emotion management is not *necessarily* immoral. The person who pretends to be excited about a birthday gift is probably not trying to "swindle" anyone. Quite the contrary. A grandchild who fakes or exaggerates gratitude may be exerting themselves in large part to protect the feelings of a beloved grandparent. Arguably, such kindness is exceedingly moral, despite the deception.

A further complexity centers on the uncertainty and ambivalence we can feel about our own beliefs and emotions. Sometimes, we do not know exactly what we think or feel about things. There are many perspectives we can adopt as we evaluate a situation, each generating a different emotional response. A person may waiver between two interpretations of an undesired present—"It's the thought that counts!" and "What a horrible gift!"—without settling on a single truth. Thus, our efforts to distinguish between honest and dishonest emotion management may sometimes involve a questionable assumption: that we know with certainty the way we really feel (Jacobsen 2023a).

On the other hand, it is definitely possible for us to underestimate the level of dishonesty that we exhibit in our emotional reactions, due to the subtlety of surface and deep acting. Yes, some of our interactions are obviously and blatantly managed, with a great deal of conscious surface and deep acting. And, on other occasions, our feelings seem to flow spontaneously, without apparent modification (Hallett 2003). However, the difference between managed and spontaneous interactions is not a dramatic on/off switch, but a matter of degree. Near the spontaneous end of the spectrum, we may engage in some very subtle, rapidly executed, and unself-conscious emotion management, such as when we habitually fake a smile or deftly work up enthusiasm without putting much thought into it. Unless people have subjected themselves to systematic self-observation (Rodriguez and Ryave 2002), they may not fully appreciate the degree to which they modify and potentially "falsify" their emotions.

Exercises

1 Describe at least one example of surface acting and one example of deep acting that you have performed. Be concrete and detailed: what specific

surface and deep acting techniques did you use? What emotional states were you attempting to feign, foster, or suppress? You could also explain why you engaged in this behavior. Were you conforming to an emotion norm, and/or attempting to accomplish some other objective?

2 Describe at least one example of interpersonal emotion management that you have observed among your classmates, friends, or relatives. Explain whose emotions were being jointly "worked on," why, and how. Was the management relatively collaborative or adversarial? Honest or dishonest?

Notes

1 As others have done (Kemper 2000:51), I treat "emotion management" and "emotion work" as higher level categories that encompass both surface acting and deep acting. This can be confusing, because Hochschild (1979:551, n2) originally used these terms as synonyms for deep acting. As with all concepts, it's important to notice the different meanings that the same terms can be given, depending on the author and the context (Harris 2022, ch. 3). To me, it makes sense to call surface and deep acting "emotion management," since my goal is to contrast (a) the active effort people put into shaping experiences and expressions of feelings, with (b) the assumptions (which I critiqued in Chapter 1) that emotions are simply instinctive, automatic, irrational, and so on. My definition of emotion management leads directly into Chapter 5's definition of emotional labor, which occurs when people are paid to engage in emotion management (surface and deep acting) as part of their job.

2 Enter the words "Texas Roadhouse shirt" into a search on Google Images, or see www.texasroadhouse.com.

3 Here an interesting connection can be made with the popular terms "comfort food" and "mood food." Both expressions imply that eating can be a form of deep acting.

4 Of course, I do not mean to imply that people deep act only for their own benefit. Deep acting is frequently done to conform to social norms and to shape the thoughts, feelings, and actions of the people who witness the results of our deep acting.

5 For more information on 4-H, see https://4-h.org/programs/agriculture/ (downloaded August 11, 2023).

Suggested Readings

In *The Managed Heart*, Hochschild provides some fascinating examples of surface and deep acting. She also discusses the ways that emotion management can be institutionalized—that is, coordinated by churches, hospitals, schools, prisons, and companies.

Hochschild, Arlie Russell. 1983. "Managing Feeling." Chapter 3 in *The Managed Heart*. Berkeley, CA: University of California Press.

Researchers have shown emotion management to be an integral part of a wide range of everyday settings, such as school, sports, support groups, intimate relationships, and fleeting interactions with strangers. Some scholars have examined how emotion management figures into politics, inequality, and social movements. Readers have a large number of options to choose from, and my follow their interests almost wherever they lead, by using the papers I've cited in this chapter, the recommended readings below, or the website Google Scholar.

Cahill, Spencer E. and Robin Eggleston. 1994. "Managing Emotions in Public: The Case of Wheelchair Users." *Social Psychology Quarterly* 57:300–312. https://doi.org/10.2307/2787157

Froyum, Carissa M. 2010. "The Reproduction of Inequalities through Emotional Capital: The Case of Socializing Low-Income Black Girls." *Qualitative Sociology* 33:37–54. https://doi.org/10.1007/s11133-009-9141-5

Lois, Jennifer. 2001. "Managing Emotions, Intimacy, and Relationships in a Volunteer Search and Rescue Group." *Journal of Contemporary Ethnography* 30:131–179. https://doi.org/10.1177/089124101030002001

Norgaard, Kari Marie. 2006. "'People Want to Protect Themselves a Little Bit': Emotions, Denial, and Social Movement Nonparticipation." *Sociological Inquiry* 76:372–396. https://doi.org/10.1111/j.1475-682X.2006.00160.x

Pearce, Jessica S. 2019. "Managing Emotion Online." *Emotion, Space and Society* 33:1–7. https://doi.org/10.1016/j.emospa.2019.100618

Wolkomir, Michelle. 2001. "Emotion Work, Commitment, and the Authentication of the Self: The Case of Gay and Ex-Gay Christian Support Groups." *Journal of Contemporary Ethnography* 30:305–334. https://doi.org/10.1177/089124101030003002

David Shulman offers a clear overview of the metaphor "Life as Theater," which undergirds the concepts of surface and deep acting. From a dramaturgical point of view (Goffman 1959), everyday life consists of actors, audiences, costumes, props, rehearsals, scripts, front stages, and back stages.

Shulman, David. 2016. *The Presentation of Self in Contemporary Social Life*. Thousand Oaks, CA: Sage.

4 Exchanging Emotions

If you're like me, then some mornings arrive sooner than you'd prefer. The alarm rings, and you're tempted to hit "snooze." You think about how great it would feel to turn off the alarm completely and return to a deep sleep.

What keeps us from doing that? One way to answer is to treat our behavior as the result of a cost–benefit calculation. However quickly or selectively, we might consider some of the good and bad outcomes that would result from alternative courses of action. How much trouble would oversleeping cause, compared to how nice it would feel?

Here the term "trouble" glosses many kinds of "costs." For example, sleepy undergraduates might worry that ignoring the alarm could have a negative impact on their understanding of course material, their course grade, their reputation with instructors and with classmates, or even their future success after college. On the other hand, the "benefits" could be manifold as well. Some extra sleep would feel good, but also might make a student happier, healthier, and more productive during the rest of the day. What to do?

A person making this sort of decision is not likely to pull out a piece of paper, compose lists of "pros" and "cons," and assess which list is longer or more persuasive. In fact, the costs and benefits may appear merely as fleeting images or half-formed sentences, or even remain "behind the scenes" as taken for granted assumptions, throughout the decision-making process. Nevertheless, the student is (arguably) acting like a *rational hedonist*. However imperfectly, they are weighing costs and benefits in order to pursue lines of action that seem pleasurable or advantageous. These cost and benefits are complex: they can be short term or long term; tangible or symbolic; clear cut or shifting and indeterminate.

Exchange Theory

The notion that human beings are rational hedonists comes from exchange theory (Rigney 2001, ch. 6). According to this perspective, virtually all social behavior can be analyzed through the prism of economic concepts. Human beings are constantly trading goods and services, in ways that seem eerily

DOI: 10.4324/b23334-4

similar to what occurs in the formal economy. As crude or abhorrent as it may sound, people often seem to "shop around" for a "good deal" when they choose their friends and romantic partners, just as they might shop for food or a new computer (Homans 1958; Hatfield 2009; Waller 1937). When deciding what to eat for lunch, we consider how expensive a restaurant is, the quality of the food it serves, how long it takes to order and receive the food, and so on. Similarly, when selecting a friend to spend time with, we may think about the various traits our friends possess (e.g., sense of humor, listening skills) and their location (e.g., a short walk or a long drive across town) before making a "purchase" by spending time with someone. If we have a bad meal or a boring hang-out session, then we may recognize the *opportunity cost* of our choice: "I could have spent my money at that other restaurant or my time with a different friend!"

Declining marginal utility (DMU) is another concept that can be imported from the business realm to social life more generally (Rigney 2001:108). In an economic setting, DMU refers to the tendency for subsequent purchases of a product to be less valued or useful than initial ones. Imagine individuals who purchase their first television for their apartment; that is likely (for many people) a major improvement and source of great satisfaction. A second television for the bedroom may come in handy but makes less of an impact. A third and fourth television—for the kitchen and bathroom—provide even smaller amounts of utility or might just get in the way.

Similarly, the same might be said of noncommercial goods and services, such as friendships, compliments, and sexual intercourse. We tend to be less incentivized to seek out new friends the more we already have. One's first (or second, third) friendship may be more highly valued than the addition of a seventeenth companion. And, while a few compliments (e.g., regarding one's appearance or career success) might be highly rewarding, a frequently praised person may come to experience such comments as virtually meaningless—if not as annoying costs rather than benefits. Picture a major celebrity like Beyoncé or Dwayne "The Rock" Johnson: the work of repeatedly expressing humility and gratitude may outweigh the negligible increase in self-esteem that they would gain from yet-another compliment. Even the value of sexual intercourse can decline, as a person accumulates more experiences and opportunities, whether premarital or marital (Blau 1964; Liu 2003).

Online behavior too, can be analyzed through exchange theory. Consider a frequent poster to Facebook, Twitter, or Instagram. They are investing their time and energy in their account. Whether they continue to do so depends on whether it is a "good deal": Am I getting enough of a "payout" in terms of attention, positive feedback, relationships, useful information, and so on? If not, they may stop and switch to another platform or to another kind of activity entirely. Or, imagine someone who feels cheated after they followed or "liked" a connection who did not "pay them back" by doing the same. Sometimes people seem to keep track of who is doing what for whom, online; depending on the nature of the relationship, there can be an implicit assumption that "I'll boost your numbers if you boost mine" and "I'll comment on your feed but you should do the same for me" (cf. Surma 2016). "Likes" can be seen as "offerings that are traded for affective and material gain" (Arcy 2016:2).

Exchange theory bothers some of my students, for good reasons. They wonder whether everyone is indeed a rational hedonist, all the time. Can't human beings behave altruistically on some occasions? For example, parents usually devote huge amounts of time, effort, and money to their children; activists may devote much of their lives to a cause. Both groups seem relatively selfless. In response, an exchange theorist might argue that parents may gain love, a valued identity ("mother" or "father"), connections to friends and relatives through children's activities (e.g., sports, school, church), and support in old age (see Nomaguchi and Milkie 2003). Activists, too, may derive much satisfaction from the influence, reputation, or legacy that their efforts yield. From a rather ruthless perspective, people volunteer for seemingly costly activities only when the return on investment is perceived as profitable or a good deal (Wilson 2000:222).

On the other hand, there is no reason to adopt such a strict orientation and impose it onto ourselves and the people around us. People are diverse and complicated. Not everyone takes a self-centered point of view, all the time. People can use a wide range of perspectives to guide their conduct (Blumer 1969:53). For example, individuals can perform actions out of duty, loyalty, love, conviction, habit, and so on, without necessarily asking "What's in it for me?" Also, selfishness–selflessness can be seen as a continuum, and over the course of a day a single person might engage in relatively self-centered acts as well as relatively altruistic acts (Haski-Leventhal 2009:290).

In an attempt to address the issue of altruism, Candace Clark (1997, 2004) differentiates three "exchange logics" that may shape people's behavior: the principle of complementary role requirements (or "complementarity"), the principle of beneficence, and the principle of reciprocity.[1] The *principle of complementarity* holds that "people should give to others because their social roles oblige them to do so" (Clark 1997:134). According to this logic, parents provide time, effort, and money to their children because they believe they are supposed to, not because of a cost–benefit calculation. Children too, as a part of their roles, might feel they owe obedience, loyalty, love, and support to their parents, simply as a matter of social obligation. Thus, a behavior may seem natural or appropriate because that's simply what a family member does. The *principle of beneficence*, in turn, "calls for giving to others who are in need, whatever their statuses or their abilities or inclinations to reciprocate" (Clark 1997:134). Here, one might donate time or money to the poor, or provide assistance to victims of a natural disaster, without worrying about being "paid back" in any way. Lastly, the *principle of reciprocity* "holds that people who give are entitled to returns, perhaps even a 'profit'" (Clark 1997:134). This principle maps the business world onto noncommercial relations: Just as a grocery store expects money in exchange for the loaf of bread, people may expect to be "reimbursed" for the favors or benefits they provide to others.

Articulating these three principles can help us see—or at least consider—that people may not think like pure exchange theorists, all the time. People may act out of complementarity (i.e., role obligations) or beneficence (i.e., altruism) rather than a self-interested concern with reciprocity. Moreover, people may switch from one logic to another, or blend multiple logics, as they navigate their relationships. Clark (1997:139) argues that Americans most frequently use two blended types of exchange logics: *reciprocal complementarity* with family members and *reciprocal beneficence* with nonkin. In each case, people act out of duty or conviction, but only up to a point. For example, we may provide what we think is "unconditional love" to a relative, but if they treat us badly too many times, then we may sever the relationship or at least cut back on the benefits we provide them (e.g., emotional support, material assistance). We discover that there were indeed strings or conditions attached to our love—we will carry out our role only so long as our relatives adequately perform their roles as well (Clark 1997:139). Similarly, reciprocal beneficence operates on the logic of "help those in need," but expects something in return, such as gratitude, respect, or favors-in-kind. You might "Of course!" help a neighbor whose house burned down, providing emotional support and a temporary place to sleep. But imagine your neighbor never expresses appreciation for your assistance, or neglects to offer emotional or material support when you lose your job two years later. The next time a major or minor tragedy strikes your neighbor, you may not feel as beneficent due to the lack of reciprocity. Or, consider volunteers who graciously serve at a soup kitchen. Such generous individuals may still feel cheated if the clientele rudely complain about the quantity, taste, or timeliness of the food (Stein 1989). When volunteers expect gratitude and respect from those they serve, it suggests that they are concerned with reciprocity in addition to beneficence.

Four Connections between Exchange Theory and Emotions

Exchange theory encourages us to consider whether cost–benefit analyses may be subtly guiding even the "loving" behavior of our family, friends, co-workers, and acquaintances, as well as ourselves. However, to appreciate and apply this perspective, it is not necessary to adopt all its tenets or treat it as universally applicable. Some people and some situations may be more amenable to cost–benefit calculations than others. If we accept that the perspective has some merit, and that people do adopt the principle of reciprocity on at least some occasions, then we can investigate the general implications exchange theory has for the study of emotion. How might emotions figure into people's sense of interactional fairness or justice? Numerous connections could be drawn (Hegtvedt and Parris 2014; Lawler and Thye 1999; Walster, Walster, and Berscheid 1978). In what follows, I will focus on four basic points.

1) Social Exchanges Produce Emotional Outcomes

One way that emotions and exchange theory intertwine is through the reactions people have *after* their exchanges: Did I get a good deal or a bad deal? Perceptions of fairness and unfairness tend to provoke particular feelings (Hatfield, Rapson, and Aumer-Ryan 2008).

For example, people often react negatively when they think they have been under-compensated. Imagine a classmate were to frequently borrow your notes but decline to share any of theirs (perhaps because of their "privacy" concerns). Over time, you might start to feel angry at being exploited. Or, if a classmate were to borrow your notes and say "Wow, your handwriting is terrible and your ideas are totally disorganized!" then you might feel especially annoyed. After all, you provided a service (the benefit of free notes) and received criticism (a cost) in return.

On the other hand, imagine a more reciprocal exchange: You lend notes one week and when you ask your classmate to do the same for you two weeks later, they say "Sure, absolutely!" This interaction may generate a feeling of satisfaction or even happiness due to the bond that was strengthened. A service has been repaid and a mutually beneficial relationship has been established.

Being over-compensated is the third option. Sometimes we think we are taking more than we are giving—such as when we constantly need to borrow notes from a friend, but never find ourselves in a position to reciprocate (perhaps because our friend is never absent). In such a situation, we might feel guilty, and search for some way to reimburse our classmate. We might ask "Can I buy you lunch?"[2]

In short, one connection between emotions and exchange theory can be seen when we focus on the feelings that follow our transactions. Fair and unfair exchanges tend to lead to particular kinds of emotional reactions, such as anger, satisfaction, or guilt. Emotions are sometimes the consequences or *outcomes* of relatively rational calculations regarding the distribution of costs and benefits in social interaction.

2) Emotions Are Factored into Cost–Benefit Analyses, as Inputs

Emotions are not only "outputs" or the results of exchange calculations. Feelings are routinely factored into cost–benefit analyses, as "inputs." For example, when contemplating whether to purchase a decadent dessert, we may consider how much money it costs, the amount of time it takes to obtain the product, and its potentially negative impact on our health. But in addition to these sorts of factors, we may also take into account feelings—such as the fleeting happiness the dessert will likely give us or the disappointment we anticipate feeling due to failing our weight-loss goals.

Similarly, students who compare different career paths may certainly consider "objective" criteria, including the potential salary and the years of schooling required. However, they may also try to imagine the emotions that different occupations may produce. Will I be proud of my job—and will my friends and relatives? Will customers and co-workers treat me with respect, rudeness, or indifference? Does one career involve more anxiety and stress than another? Here emotions factor into the calculation of whether pursuing an occupation would be a good deal (i.e., worth the investment of time, effort, and money).

Let's reconsider the example of students who swap class notes. If a classmate says "Wow, thanks, your notes are excellent," then perhaps a brief feeling of pride is factored into an overall calculation regarding the fairness of the exchange. Someone may be willing to continue to loan notes several times in a row, in exchange for expressions of praise and gratitude, because the positive emotions those displays generate make the transaction seem fair, or at least fair enough. On the other hand, a comment such as "Your notes are dumb!" may produce embarrassment; this uncomfortable feeling could be considered a "cost" that makes the exchange unfair and thus undesirable to continue in the future.

In short, a second basic connection between exchange theory and emotions is this: we take our feelings into account when we calculate the "profitability" of a potential activity. Emotions are among the costs and the benefits that we tally up as we decide whether to undertake a course of action. Too many emotional costs may lead us to stop pursuing a relationship, hobby, major, or career, despite the existence of other (more concrete or "objective") benefits.

3) People May "Work On" the Emotions They Exchange with Others

Treating emotions as inputs and outputs of cost–benefit calculations can be illuminating. However, there is a risk: that approach can lead us to overlook the dynamic nature of our feelings. Emotions are not static entities (like televisions or dollar bills) that we may accumulate or dispense. Feelings are not merely experiences that happen to us. Rather, human beings can actively modify their emotions—through surface and deep acting—as they engage in exchanges with others (Hochschild 1983:82–83).

When borrowing notes, for example, students may feign or exaggerate emotions in order to "pay back" the note-taker. Individuals can purposefully modify their wording, tone, and facial expressions as they enthusiastically exclaim "Thank you so much!" even though the notes were not very helpful. Deference can be faked or inflated as well. A student may describe mediocre notes as "Really excellent" or "So much better than my own notes!" in order to exchange a compliment (a gift of pride) for the free assistance.

Deep acting may also come into play. After borrowing and copying some shoddy class notes, a student may feel frustrated: *This wasn't very helpful. I doubt I would be able to answer an essay question on this material!* By focusing on opportunity costs, frustration may even turn to anger: *I shouldn't have wasted my time borrowing notes from Joe. I should have asked Maria when I had the chance!* To escape these negative emotions, the student might use cognitive deep acting to suppress annoyance and evoke gratitude: *Well, at least it's good to have a general idea what material was covered in class. The odds are slim that there will be an essay question on this. It was nice of Joe to offer up his notes to me so quickly, even if they weren't as helpful as I hoped.*

Thus, we can link concepts from Chapter 3 on emotion management to our understanding of exchange theory here in Chapter 4. People may sometimes treat their emotions as inputs and outputs of exchange calculations, but those emotions can be "worked on" and modified at any time—before, during, or after a transaction.

4) Emotional Exchanges Occur against the Backdrop of Emotion Norms and Other Cultural Beliefs

Regardless of whether surface or deep acting is used, notice that our exchanges take place within the context of cultural expectations—the subject of Chapter 2. When someone provides the gift of free notes, the receiver is generally expected to express gratitude. To say nothing would violate an emotion norm, which might prompt sanctions from one's classmates. However, at the same time, both participants to the exchange are keeping track of whether they are getting a fair deal, and their assessments shape their emotions and their actions—including whether to engage in a similar interaction with each other in the future.

According to Hochschild (1983:76), emotion norms set a kind of "baseline" for social exchange. A certain level of gratitude may be expected upon receiving a favor. A display that exceeds this level (in intensity or duration) can often seem like a "gift"—as when someone says "Thank you so much!!!" instead of a milder "Thanks." The amount of gratitude that exceeds the norm may feel especially rewarding, which would be a "plus" that is factored into the giver's cost–benefit calculations. On the other hand, an excessive display of gratitude or deference could also be taken as patronizing. A two-minute speech on the quality of the note-taker's handwriting may be received as excessive to the point of mockery, producing feelings of embarrassment or annoyance that become "costs" rather than "benefits." Norms about the intensity and duration of gratitude can influence perceptions about its value in an interpersonal exchange.[3]

Similarly, other cultural beliefs can impact the calculations people make during their exchanges with others. For example, children are assumed to be less responsible for their actions and emotions than adults are. Thus, they are often given a great amount of leeway in their interactions. A young child can extract emotions from others—sympathy, love, expressions of kindness and patience—without necessarily being required to reciprocate in the short or long term (Clark 1997:155). On the other hand, women may be expected to generate larger emotional gifts, due to assumptions that emotions come more easily to them. A female paralegal, for instance, may receive less credit than a male paralegal would for displays of a supportive and upbeat demeanor.

Supervising lawyers may simply expect such behavior from female employees, rather than treating it as a "gift" (Pierce 1995). Finally, in many but not all cultures, customer service workers are frequently expected to generate expressions of positive emotions ("Welcome to the Gap!") as part of their paid employment, even if customers do not repay those expressions in kind. Any emotional inequality in the relationship between customers and workers is assumed to be rectified by one's wage (Hochschild 1983:86).

Spotlight on Research

Exchanging Sympathy in the Socioemotional Economy

Candace Clark's (1997) book *Misery and Company* provides the most interesting, thorough, and accessible example of the application of exchange theory to emotions. To investigate the role of sympathy in American culture, Clark collected data from a variety of sources. She (and her assistants) conducted ninety-three in-depth interviews, administered a survey to over 1,200 respondents, observed and participated in sympathy exchanges in a variety of natural settings (e.g., hospitals, funeral parlors, offices), and collected written expressions of sympathy that appeared in greeting cards and news reports. Less formally, she collected data through intensive eavesdropping, focused conversations, and (as a way to prompt further reflection by respondents) guided freewriting. In addition, Clark read fictional and nonfictional work on sympathy and sympathetic characters, and engaged in careful introspection (Ellis 1991), to examine her own reactions. Clark's eclectic methodology gave her numerous vantage points on a complex and subtle topic.

Based on her analysis of these materials, Clark found that sympathy was shaped by rational calculations and a variety of social factors. Every person has a *sympathy biography*—a history or pattern of giving and receiving sympathy. Their prior conduct shapes how many sympathy credits that they have in their *sympathy accounts*. Individuals who fail to reciprocate sympathy would risk their credit rating with others. Thus, if a good friend comforts you after a difficult breakup, but two months later you can't be bothered to return the favor, then your friend may not respond to any of your requests in the future. Or, picture a person who makes unwarranted claims to sympathy, by exaggerating or lying about personal problems. While Americans might appreciate someone who prompts amusement by making silly jokes, they tend to experience silly requests for sympathy as an unnecessary and offensive "cost." Thus, telling dubious tales of woe can quickly deplete sympathy accounts, since false claims are even more "expensive" than true ones. Eventually people will stop listening and conveying support.

On the other hand, a person who always gives and never receives sympathy may also run into trouble. Rather than building up a huge reserve of sympathy credits, such individuals risk having their accounts closed altogether. A person who never needs sympathy may alienate others, by appearing too aloof, superior, or self-sufficient. Consequently, when a calamity does strike, others may assume or tell the individual "You'll be fine, just like you always are." An inactive sympathy account may be closed by one's companions just like an unused credit card may be canceled by one's bank.

Sympathy accounts are also affected by interpretations of individuals' *social worth*. That is, "people view some categories of social actors as more valuable, worthwhile, or important than others" (Clark 1997:114). Human beings draw somewhat artificial boundaries when they assign sympathy accounts to members of their family, community, race, religion, or nation. People cannot generate limitless expressions of sympathy, and so they make arbitrary—yet culturally informed—decisions about whom to support emotionally and materially. Social worth is determined by membership in valued groups as well as by the perceived causes of one's predicaments. Individuals who are deemed to suffer from "bad luck" are given more leeway than those who are perceived as bringing trouble upon themselves. Thus, an alcoholic might now be interpreted as suffering an unfortunate disease, whereas in an earlier era he might have accrued more blame (and less sympathy) for his problems (Clark 1997:109).

In these and other ways, Clark argued that sympathy flows through a *socioemotional economy*—a system that is shaped by normative understandings of proper behavior as well as rational calculations regarding expenditures and revenue (see also Clark 1987).

Can you apply Clark's ideas to your own life? Can you think of a time when your sympathy biography added to, or subtracted from, your sympathy account?

Misgivings and Ambivalence: Conflicting Interpretations of Emotional Exchanges

In the realm of commerce, people do not always agree on the value of things. Sometimes, a customer may think that they have been overcharged for a product or service. Or, a salesperson and a customer may not be able to reach agreement on the price of a new automobile or used guitar, leading to an aborted transaction or to one party feeling cheated by the other. Thus, the business analogy that undergirds exchange theory (Rigney 2001) can be extended further to help illustrate a final point about emotions and exchange theory.

Like commercial transactions, informal and non-monetary exchanges can also involve disagreements—or *misgivings*—over the value of the goods and services that people trade with each other (Hochschild 2003). Misgivings can affect people's emotional experiences, displays, and management, regardless of whether such discrepancies are explicitly acknowledged and discussed.

To illustrate this notion, let's return to the example of an undesirable birthday present. A grandparent may spend a substantial amount of time searching for, purchasing, and wrapping a sweater for a grandchild. The thought, effort, and money that went into the present may endow it with a significance or value that is not recognized by the grandchild, who only sees "an ugly sweater I'll never wear." The grandchild may feign a moderate amount of gratitude, in order to conform to emotion rules and protect the feelings of the grandparent. And this surface acting may seem like a "gift" or a "repayment" from the perspective of the grandchild, since effort is being expended to repay a totally undesirable birthday present. However, the grandparent may still detect a hint of disappointment or a lower level of enthusiasm than was expected, given the presumed value of the gift. As a result, both may feel cheated or disrespected by the exchange. Even though neither person openly discusses the issue, the relationship can be damaged rather than strengthened.

"Gifts" can include not only wrapped presents, but less tangible favors as well. Big and small transactions occur on a routine basis between close companions, such as two college roommates. Picture an *extrovert*—a person who thrives on social interaction and verbal communication with others—living alongside an *introvert*—someone who enjoys conversation only in small doses (Cain 2012). An extrovert may enthusiastically ask "How was your day?" as soon as the introvert walks in the door. This gesture may be intended as a benefit—an expression of interest and affection, and a willingness to listen to the concerns of the other. However, the introvert may experience this behavior as a cost, since her preference is to have a bit of quiet solitude at the end of a long day. Similarly, the extrovert may plan a surprise birthday party for her roommate, not realizing that what seemed like a generous present to her would be an unwelcomed burden to her introverted companion. The introvert may need to deep or surface act her way through the party, and through any expressions of gratitude to her roommate. If the introvert expresses anger—either out of exhaustion or exasperation over being misunderstood—then she may be judged harshly for violating an emotion norm and for not repaying the presumed gift her roommate gave her.

Interpersonal commodities can be priced at different levels by different people, or even by a single person. As odd as it may sound, individuals can disagree with themselves, or not have "one mind" regarding a particular topic. Sometimes we can feel ambivalent, wavering between two or more points of view (Jacobsen 2023a). For example, an introvert may be unable to decide how she feels about a surprise party that an extrovert roommate threw. *Was it simply overwhelming and "too much," or was it good for me to be surrounded by a gathering of friends? Did my roommate act insensitively by misunderstanding my preferences, or was she just being thoughtful and generous?* Through cognitive deep acting, the introvert may try to talk herself into a feeling that conforms to emotion norms and repays an apparent debt. On the other hand, she may focus on thoughts that lead to more anger and conflict with her roommate.

People's perspectives are neither monolithic nor permanent. The value that a person places on an interpersonal commodity can evolve over time. Consider one gift that a romantic partner trade with another: washing the dishes. The value placed on this activity is not necessarily static and may change as the relationship evolves (Nelson 2011). For example, a boyfriend may receive an enthusiastic "Thanks so much!" from his girlfriend for doing the dishes at her apartment; then, after cautiously moving in together, the same man may receive a milder "Thanks"; then, years later as a husband, the same man may receive almost no recognition, since his wife (quite reasonably) considers him equally responsible for housework. The man may be perplexed. *"I'm the same person, doing the same chore, but I get no gratitude for it! Why doesn't my wife appreciate me the way she used to?"* A man who is not sensitive to the changing value of gifts may not notice or understand that the "going rate" for washing dishes has changed. His wife once priced dishwashing as a favor but now considers it a duty.

Exercises

Recall a social exchange that has occurred between you and a friend, co-worker, or relative. Consider two or more of the following questions:

1 Did emotions play a role in the exchange, as outcomes or as inputs?
2 Did you or your companion use surface or deep acting during the exchange?
3 Did emotion norms shape your conduct and/or your rational calculations?
4 Were there any misgivings or ambivalence within the transaction?

Notes

1 In articulating these logics, Clark builds on the work of Gouldner (1973) and other scholars.
2 Of course, some people may be narcissists or may derive a sneaky thrill from taking advantage of others, which may encourage them to continue their exploitive behavior until sanctions (costs) are imposed or the relationship ends.
3 When analyzing social interaction, it can be difficult to decide how to interpret people's behavior. Are actors simply conforming to social norms? Are they making rational calculations in order to select the more profitable courses of action? It is often a judgment call whether to emphasize one prism, or both, or neither, when making sense of human behavior. As I mentioned in Chapter 1, the concepts we discuss in this book are tools you can use to understand yourself and the world around you—but the tools must be creatively tested out, rather than robotically memorized and applied.

Suggested Readings

In the fifth chapter of *The Managed Heart*, Hochschild (1983:78) explains her famous assertion that "we keep a mental ledger with 'owed' and 'received' columns for gratitude, love, anger, guilt, and other feelings." She also distinguishes between "straight" and "improvised" exchanges and their relationship to emotion norms. In a subsequent paper, Hochschild (2003) applies exchange principles to the division of household labor between husbands and wives. Spouses' displays of gratitude are connected to their gendered assumptions about housework and the supply of men willing to do it. Margaret Nelson (2011) builds on Hochschild's work, by highlighting connections between the *stage* of a relationship and the exchanges that take place within it.

Hochschild, Arlie Russell. 1983. "Paying Respects with Feeling: The Gift Exchange." Chapter 5 in *The Managed Heart*. Berkeley, CA: University of California Press.

Hochschild, Arlie Russell. 2003. "The Economy of Gratitude." Pp. 104–118 in *The Commercialization of Intimate Life: Notes from Home and Work*. Berkeley, CA: University of California Press.

Nelson, Margaret K. 2011. "Love and Gratitude: Single Mothers Talk about Men's Contributions to the Second Shift." Pp. 100–111 in *At the Heart of Work and Family: Engaging the Ideas of Arlie Hochschild*, edited by Anita Ilta Garey and Karen V. Hansen. New Brunswick, NJ: Rutgers.

Although written sixty years ago, Peter Blau's perspective on premarital sex remains a fascinating and readable example of exchange theory. Blau uses market principles—such as supply and demand—to explain when and why couples engage in premarital sex acts, and the conditions under which sexual favors lead to a lasting mutual attachment. Eva Illouz, in turn, compares premodern and modern procedures for selecting romantic partners. Her dense but insightful book shows how the rational calculations that pervade modern sexual behavior are shaped by larger social forces that have changed over time. Illouz thus puts exchange theory into historical perspective.

Blau, Peter M. 1964. "Excursus on Love." Pp. 76–87 in *Exchange and Power in Social Life*. New York: Wiley.

Illouz, Eva. 2012. *Why Love Hurts: A Sociological Explanation*. Cambridge: Polity. (See the second chapter, in particular.)

For those seeking more technical overviews of the connections between exchange theory and emotions, you might consider these options.

Lawler, Edward J. and Shane R. Thye. 1999. "Bringing Emotions into Social Exchange Theory." *Annual Review of Sociology* 25:217–244. https://doi.org/10.1146/annurev.soc.25.1.217

Hegtvedt, Karen A. and Christie L. Parris. 2014. "Emotions in Justice Processes." Pp. 103–125 in *Handbook of the Sociology of Emotions* (Vol. II), edited by Jan E. Stets and Jonathan H. Turner. New York: Springer.

Daniel Rigney clearly explains the metaphor "Life as Business" (or "Society as Marketplace"), which undergirds exchange theory. From this perspective, virtually any social interaction can be analyzed as if it were analogous to an economic transaction, using concepts such as profit, supply and demand, and opportunity costs.

Rigney, Daniel. 2001. "Society as Marketplace." Chapter 6 in *The Metaphorical Society: An Invitation to Social Theory*. Lanham, MD: Rowman & Littlefield.

5   Emotional Labor

So far we've discussed three social dimensions of emotion: norms, management, and exchange. In this chapter, we'll build on this backdrop as we turn to a new topic—emotional labor.

Let's ease our way into the subject by returning to the tentative distinction (discussed in Chapter 1) between thinking, acting, and feeling. By extrapolating from each term, we might distinguish (loosely) between three kinds of labor. *Cognitive labor* would draw attention to the concentration and thought that certain tasks require, such as diagnosing a disease, navigating a tax code, or bidding on a bathroom remodel. *Physical labor* highlights circumstances where people must use their strength and manual dexterity to get their jobs done, perhaps by hammering nails, lifting boxes, assembling hamburgers, or amputating gangrenous tissue. The concept of emotional labor, in turn, can help us recognize another dimension of paid employment.

Put succinctly, people perform *emotional labor* whenever they manage emotions in their occupations. Workers frequently use surface acting and deep acting in order to experience and display the feelings that their jobs require. For example, a waitress may need to suppress impatience (with slow customers), disguise boredom (due to monotony), or feign cheerful enthusiasm (when lethargic). Neither the waitress nor her employer may possess a technical vocabulary for explicitly discussing this labor, besides relatively vague expressions such as "having a good attitude" or "buttering up customers" (Hallett 2003). Nevertheless, a worker's ability and willingness to effectively perform emotional labor can determine whether she is hired or fired and can have a direct impact on the size of the tips that customers leave.

Emotional labor is most apparent in those jobs that require workers to interact directly and frequently with customers (Leidner 1999). Occupations such as hostesses, cashiers, telemarketers, and hair stylists, come to mind. Or, imagine casino card dealers: these workers engage in friendly conversation for several hours a day as they administer a game that systematically subtracts cash from customers' wallets (Enarson 1993; Sallaz 2002). People who sell cars, homes, cell phones, shoes, and other products might also engage in a great deal of emotion management (Prus 1989).

DOI: 10.4324/b23334-5

In addition to customer service and sales jobs, professional occupations also require emotional labor: accountants, lawyers, doctors, nurses, psychiatrists, social workers, and teachers all must modify their emotions in order to successfully execute their jobs (e.g., Bellas 1999; Delaney 2012; Erickson and Grove 2008; Simonova 2017). A professional who displays excessive anger or insufficient sympathy might lose clients or at least gain a bad reputation.

It is accurate but somewhat incomplete to define emotional labor as *being paid to manage one's own emotions*. In a broader sense, the concept of emotional labor also draws attention to how workers must work on *other people's* feelings as well. Many jobs require laborers to try to keep customers relatively happy or satisfied. Other jobs encourage workers to reduce customers' fear or anxiety. Imagine the confident yet consoling tone of voice that might be strategically used by nurses, flight attendants, tattoo artists, and tax attorneys. In any of these cases, the emotional laborer may go to great lengths not only to manage their own emotions, but to shape the feelings of customers and clients.

Co-workers can be targets of emotion management as well. For example, when employees compete with each other for tips, commissions, or compliments from the boss, the "losers" may need to mask their envy while the "winners" suppress the urge to gloat. An employee may be slow, incompetent, or wear an excessive amount of cologne or perfume, prompting co-workers to suppress their feelings of frustration or irritation. Many employees undergo an annual performance review, where supervisors try to convey criticisms and compliments in ways that create just the right emotional effect, while workers carefully respond. Even CEOs and small business owners need to occasionally motivate employees by engaging in emotion management—perhaps by modeling enthusiasm or by presenting an optimistic demeanor while giving a speech (Humphrey 2012).

Virtually every job requires *some* emotion management, even if little or no social interaction occurs. People who work completely alone—perhaps at a home office or inside a truck on the freeway—will probably still manage their emotions occasionally (Musson and Marsh 2008). If an isolated worker tries to overcome boredom, fend off loneliness, stifle frustration, or work up enthusiasm to finish a task, then there is likely some deep acting occurring.[1]

Four Ways Employers Influence their Employees' Emotional Labor

Not all employers concern themselves with the emotion management of their employees. Managers may fail to recognize the importance of emotional labor, or they may deem it irrelevant. When hiring welders, for example, "people skills" may seem insignificant next to competence with a torch. Similarly, an employer might forgive a toll booth operator for being surly; since drivers have no choice but to pay, a "nice personality" may not be deemed essential.

On the other hand, sometimes employers do want to hire competent emotional laborers. If a toll booth operator is considered part of the public face of a city, then emotion management may be deemed very relevant and important.

Thus, in many cases, employers do take emotional labor into account when they hire, train, and evaluate their staff (Leidner 1999). Let's examine these three strategies for controlling emotional labor, along with a more indirect means by which employers affect emotional labor—advertising (Hochschild 1983).

1) Hiring

I doubt a single employer has ever placed this announcement in the "help wanted" section of a newspaper or on a corporate website:

> Wanted: worker who can use surface and deep acting to generate company-preferred emotional experiences and displays.

Less technical terminology, however, may be used to convey similar ideas. In the want ads of local newspapers, employers seek workers who possess positive attitudes, strong interpersonal skills, outgoing or friendly personalities, and the ability to work well with others. Kotchemidova (2005) searched Monster.com and found 200 different jobs that required applicants to have a "cheerful personality." Humorously, in Oregon I once saw an advertisement for a cook who possessed "no ego"—a strict prerequisite indeed! (Perhaps only accomplished Buddhists need apply.) Arguably, these sorts of descriptions imply some concern with employee's ability to present appropriate emotional displays, either "naturally" or through surface and deep acting.

After applying for an advertised position, job candidates may be interviewed with emotion management skills as an implicit criterion. Applicants may be asked to respond to hypothetical scenarios ("How would you respond if...") or to recount examples of emotionally challenging situations they've handled in the past. The interview setting itself can serve as a test of sorts.[2] In Hochschild's (1983:4) research on flight attendants, one airline gathered six applicants in a room and encouraged them to get to know each other while they waited. Candidates could then be secretly watched and evaluated for their ability to engage in friendly conversation with strangers. Or, consider potential firefighters (Scott and Myers 2005). Applicants for this position participate in ride-alongs to learn about the job; at the same time, department members subtly observe and evaluate the candidate's people skills (e.g., ability to cope with stress and act congenially with the public and co-workers), in order to weed out those with inferior emotion management skills.

Not all employers go to such lengths. However, even if an interview consists of a simple impromptu conversation, an employer may still be attempting to discern "what applicants are like"—which (in part) may mean "Can this person at least fake appropriate emotional displays?"

2) Training

Employees may be hired for their pre-existing emotion management skills, but things can still go wrong. For example, after interacting with an especially rude customer, even the most "naturally" cheerful waiters or salespeople may experience frustration or anger that exceeds the emotion management skills they brought to their jobs. To prevent this situation, employers may train workers (explicitly or implicitly) to use company-approved strategies for surface and deep acting (Leidner 1999).[3]

Surface acting is encouraged when employees are given simple instructions about facial expressions and physical gestures, such as "Your smile is your biggest asset—use it" (Hochschild 1983:105) and "Never display any body language that could be interpreted as negative or unfriendly" (Sallaz 2002:407). By watching orientation videos, a new employee may learn the correct wording and tone of voice to use. Workers may be trained to say "Goodbye! Thanks for coming! Hope to see you soon!" regardless of whether they feel gratitude or an eagerness to interact with a particular shopper again. New employees may be given advice (if not strict regulations) regarding their hair, makeup, jewelry, and clothing, in order to present a particular image to the customer or maintain a degree of "professionalism" in an office (Witz et al. 2003). Arguably, a partial goal of these instructions is to ensure proper surface acting. An appearance that seems too "Goth," "Emo," "heavy metal," or simply disheveled may project feelings of sadness or anger that employers deem inappropriate.

Deep-acting instructions go further. Some employers want emotions to be actually experienced rather than merely "put on" like a mask (see Hochschild 1983:105). From the perspective of these employers, it's better to employ a worker who can actually transform irritation into more positive emotions, rather than use a fake smile to cover up irritation. To encourage workers to deep act their way into desired emotional states, a variety of cognitive tactics can be taught.

Customer service slogans might be used to engender "appropriate" (i.e., company preferred) ways of thinking and feeling among employees. Usually, employers don't want workers to get angry and argue with an unhappy customer. Instead, they want employees to feel sympathy, remorse, and excitement to serve. Consider these common expressions, which seem tailored to guiding workers in that direction:

- The customer is always right.
- There is only one boss—the customer.
- The customer is king.
- The customer's perception is your reality.
- We owe our jobs to our customers.

Slogans such as these can be seen as emotional training; employers are hoping that workers will use these thoughts to deep act their way into more profitable feelings. If the employer said "Just put on a show as if the customer is right, even when they are being grouchy, unfair, or idiotic," then that would be training employees to do surface acting.

Sometimes training goes well beyond slogans. Companies may quite purposefully socialize workers into specific ways of thinking, through an extensive training process. Leidner (1993), for example, studied an insurance company that required trainees to attend two weeks of classes (8a.m.–5p.m., plus homework). The main focus of the classes was not on the technical details of insurance products, but on sales strategies and the philosophy of PMA—positive mental attitude. Workers were instructed on ways of thinking that would produce happiness, enthusiasm, and confidence. For instance, agents were told to envision the most successful salesperson they could, and then model their attitude after that person (Leidner 1993:104). The **Spotlight on Research** in this chapter describes another case of extensive deep-acting instruction, involving college-aged salespersons (Schweingruber and Berns 2005).

Emotional training is not only top-down. Co-workers can socialize each other into the company culture, even if only in an implicit manner. When a new employee enters a workforce, they may not be explicitly told about emotion norms or management strategies. Instead, the worker may observe and learn from other employees, as when new firefighters observe senior members and try to mimic their emotional demeanor out in the field and back in the station (Scott and Myers 2005:83). Through surface or deep acting, workers may attempt to assimilate and "fit in" with the organizational culture. Those who deviate too far from expectations may be sanctioned, which we'll discuss next.

3) Monitoring and Evaluating

Not everyone is able or inclined to perform emotional labor consistently well. Even carefully hired and trained workers may fail to meet employers' expectations. Some workers may surface act their way through a job interview and an orientation period but become less enthusiastic a few days later. Or, after several months of greeting customers ("Welcome!" "Have a great day!"), even the most obedient and diligent employee may become increasingly lethargic, if not downright gruff. Arguably, some workplaces make virtually impossible demands on their emotional laborers (Copp 1998). Since poor emotional displays can negatively impact an establishment's reputation and balance sheet, employers may take steps to monitor workers' performance.

Several strategies are possible (Leidner 1999). The simplest is direct observation, where a manager watches an employee from across the room. While potentially useful, workers may behave differently when the boss is not on site or is out of view. A video camera may enable an employer to observe workers from afar, either concurrently or by reviewing the tape at a later date. Phone calls with customers may also be recorded, so that workers can be reprimanded for improper emotional displays. Some call centers use software to detect inappropriate emotional displays and automatically alert managers to intervene before a call ends badly (van Jaarsveld and Poster 2013).

The clientele can also be enlisted to provide surveillance, feedback, and sanctions. Many customers are sensitive to the subtle emotional cues that workers give off. At a restaurant, the gratuity added to the check may be tied to waiters' ability to manage emotions as much as to the quality of the food and speed of its delivery. Besides tipping, customers can make their evaluations known in written form—by filling out comment cards or responding to surveys by phone, mail, and the internet. For example, each time my car was repaired by my local Honda dealership, a surveyor called to ask about my experience, including the treatment I received from the company's staff.

Some corporations do not only rely on the feedback of regular customers. Instead, they hire people to *pretend* to be customers, in order to observe and evaluate workers' performance (Ashkanasy and Daus 2002). These "secret shoppers" can measure competence along a number of dimensions—including employees' demeanor.

Regular co-workers may also be relied upon to monitor the quality of the emotional labor that an employee provides. Conscientious (or meddling!) employees may decide to inform a manager when they notice that a co-worker has deviated from the company's emotion norms. Such feedback might occur publicly or through confidential back-room discussions.

4) Advertising

Employers guide emotional labor by strategically hiring, training, and monitoring their workers. Interestingly, and more subtly, employers can also exert an indirect influence on an employee's emotional labor through the advertising choices they make. Usually, advertising tends raise the expectations of customers, thereby increasing the amount of emotional labor that workers need to perform (Hochschild 1983:93).

In order to promote interest in a particular product or service, companies tend to promise customers a very positive experience. For example, a fast-food corporation may use advertisements implying that customers' meals will be made quickly, will look beautiful and taste delicious, and will be delivered by smiling, happy workers. In the real world, many factors may prohibit these expectations from being met—including factors beyond the control of any low-level employee. A fast-food establishment may become very busy (or be understaffed), leading to long waits, lower quality food, and frantic employees; plus, the food that appears in advertisements is a meticulously staged and nearly-impossible-to-deliver version of the product. Consequently, customers may express their dissatisfaction to employees—an uncomfortable situation exacerbated by overzealous advertising. On these occasions, workers act as *shock absorbers* for the company: they absorb (or attempt to soften) the jarring impact that unmet expectations can have (Hochschild 1983:175).

Take a look at the advertisements you see on television (and other locations), to test out these ideas for yourself. In the past few years, I have seen Walmart depict their workers as thrilled to see customers; MerryMaids cleaners portrayed as jumping for joy over their love of dusting and vacuuming; and Olive Garden waiters described as so welcoming that they treat customers like family members. Arguably, all these advertisements tend to raise customers' expectations and increase workers' emotional labor. Sometimes, advertisements highlight employees' sexuality (Hochschild 1983:93). When male customers are given the impression that female flight attendants or waitresses are sexually available, the workers may need to perform the additional emotional labor of gracefully responding to unwanted flirting or harassment.

Of course, customers don't always take advertising seriously. Not everyone's expectations are easily manipulated. However, at least *some* people are affected by advertising, and when their expectations are raised unrealistically, they may take it out on employees. Thus, decisions that employers make about advertising can have indirect but consequential effects on the emotional labor that their workers need to perform.

Spotlight on Research

Training Young Salespeople to Be Successful Emotional Laborers

Imagine you are a college student who wants a summer job. You're presented with a chance to earn thousands of dollars *more* than you could from a minimum-wage position at a fast-food restaurant. Sounds great, right? But there's a catch. Would you be willing to go door-to-door, selling educational books to parents of elementary and high school students?

Consider the challenges. Customers may repeatedly say "no," and rudely yell at you to get off their property. Your family and friends may be skeptical, raising questions about your safety and the risk of being paid by commission. And this is not a 9a.m.-to-5p.m. desk job in the air conditioning. The weather may be hot or rainy, which is no fun when walking around unfamiliar neighborhoods. Shifts last over twelve hours a day, six days a week.

Would you still be interested in earning those extra thousands of dollars? Many college students are, and they choose to sell door-to-door over the summer, for a company like this one: www.southwesternadvantage.com.

In "Shaping the Selves of Young Salespeople through Emotion Management," David Schweingruber and Nancy Berns (2005) conducted an intriguing study of student book sellers, focusing on a company they called "Enterprise" (a pseudonym). The authors collected a wide range of data on Enterprise and its staff. They observed managers and salespeople in a variety of settings (e.g., sales calls, recruiting and training sessions); they interviewed Enterprise workers, formally and informally; they analyzed company documents (such as manuals, tapes, and historical records); and they held a series of focus groups. In addition, personal experience benefitted the researchers, as Berns had served as an Enterprise salesperson for three years.

Schweingruber and Berns found that Enterprise went to great lengths to prepare its workers to engage in emotional labor. Although there were sales scripts to memorize and forms to fill out, managers considered 80 percent of the training to be emotional (p. 688). The company actually used the term "emotional training" to describe the process of enabling workers to think and feel in ways that produced endurance and effectiveness.

One strategy the company used was to require workers to develop "emotional purposes" (p. 681). Trainees were told that money was not a sufficient reason to take this difficult job. In order to enable salespeople to last and thrive through the summer, managers helped workers think of a more personalized incentive. For example, workers used their close relationships in order to set a variety of non-monetary goals—such as making their parents proud, proving that a skeptical friend was wrong, or becoming a successful role model for one's future children.

Enterprise reinforced these emotional purposes through a number of activities. Workers were told to write down their purposes, discuss them with co-workers, and repeat them aloud while walking door-to-door. The company also incorporated workers' emotional purposes into various meetings, ceremonies, and competitions. Moreover, salespeople were trained to engage in imaginary conversations with the significant others who were at the center of their emotional purposes. These conversations could be used on challenging days, to overcome frustration or fear and bolster workers' determination to succeed. (Here you might notice a parallel with the work of Shane Sharp [2010], which was discussed in Chapter 3.)

Along with emotional purposes, workers were trained to use several other emotion management strategies. One of these—a form of cognitive deep acting—was to redefine the summer job as providing a *service* rather than as merely making sales. Managers told workers that they were not simply selling widgets but were providing educational books that would help customers' children do well in school and lead richer lives. In addition, workers were taught that they could make the world a better place simply by interacting with people. Any potential customer might benefit from exposure to a friendly Enterprise salesperson, either temporarily (from being cheered up) or more permanently (from

> being exposed to a model of positivity). These instructions provided a moral foundation to the work of door-to-door sales and gave Enterprise workers another method for suppressing negative emotions, even in the face of customers' indifference and hostility.

Inequality among Emotional Laborers

Through hiring, training, monitoring, and advertising, employers exert a great amount of control over their workers. However, workers do have some power. For example, they can "fool" those who do the hiring and training, by saying and doing whatever it takes to get the job and then performing it as they see fit. Monitoring too, is imperfect, and workers can evade a company's emotion norms occasionally. In some instances, workers may even "push back" or rebel against employers' efforts to organize their emotions (Rodriquez 2011). Nevertheless, those who have the power to hire and fire usually have the most power, and their employees know it.

Inequality impacts emotional labor in another way—through differences among workers. Not everyone is expected to do the same amount of emotional labor. Some workers' surface and deep acting can be more frequent, intense, and grueling, depending on their gender, race, and status.

Gender

If emotional labor were gender-neutral, then men and women would perform it equally. Sociologists have argued that this is not the case (Bellas 2001). Instead, female workers tend to do more emotional labor than male workers. This is because (a) occupations can be segregated by gender; (b) tasks within an occupation can be segregated by gender; and (c) female workers can receive differential treatment even when doing the same task within the same occupation.

Occupations are segregated because certain career paths tend to be dominated by men or by women. Those jobs that require additional emotional labor are often considered "women's work." For example, pilots tend to be male whereas flight attendants are more likely to be female. The latter job clearly involves greater opportunities for emotional labor. Flight attendants are more likely to deal with passengers who are scared to fly, worried about lost luggage, or angered over a late departure. Only in rare and extreme circumstances do pilots involve themselves in controlling passengers' emotions and conduct, beyond making announcements over the loudspeaker.

Similar patterns can be seen in other settings (Guy and Newman 2004). While not ironclad laws, gendered tendencies can be found in restaurants, hospitals, and corporations. Women are more likely to serve as waitresses, nurses, and receptionists, and thus interact more directly with the public than cooks, doctors, and executives do. In all these instances, women tend to gravitate or are guided towards those roles that require more emotional labor. Very few men become elementary school teachers (where much nurturing is required) and very few women become construction workers (where the labor is more physical than emotional).[4]

Of course, few if any occupations are completely segregated by gender. There are some male nurses, receptionists, and elementary school teachers. Yet even when men and women hold the same job, there can still be *segregation by tasks* within a position (Bellas 2001). A male flight attendant might be asked to lift a heavy bag into an overhead compartment more often, but a female flight attendant is more likely to face requests for emotional labor—such as providing comfort to children, the elderly, or the bereaved. Women who have successfully broken into the realm of policing may find that the job is not the same for a man as it is for a woman. When it comes to consoling victims of sex crimes and other offenses, female police officers may be expected to take the lead (Martin 1999).

If *occupations* and *tasks within occupations* were both distributed randomly, then in both cases we would expect to see a near 50–50 division among the sexes. However, such a gender-neutral scenario would still not guarantee that men and women performed similar amounts of emotional labor. This is because even when male and female employees perform the same task within the same occupation, *the behavior of customers, co-workers, and employers can still increase the demands placed on women* (Bellas 2001). For example, when a female flight attendant reminds passengers to buckle their seat belts or store loose luggage under their seats, customers may feel freer to express irritation or resistance—especially those who are less inclined to recognize women as authority figures or who assume that women are naturally more nurturing (Hochschild 1983:174). A female waitress or receptionist is more likely to need to politely fend off an unwanted sexual advance or harassment from a customer, compared to a male counterpart in the same occupation. Or, students may expect their female teachers to be more sympathetic and warm than their male teachers (Bellas 1999).

In addition to customers, co-workers and employers may expect female employees to be kinder and friendlier than their male counterparts who hold the same position. A co-worker who needs to vent about an irritating customer, or a boss who wants to see a broad smile or nurturing tone during a hallway conversation, may hold higher expectations for staff members who are women (e.g., see Pierce 1999).

The gendered nature of women's employment mirrors the unpaid work that women do at home. In many families, women tend to do more of the housework and the "kin work"—nurturing children, caring for elderly parents, planning gatherings, fostering conversations, and the like (Chavez, Paige, and Edelblute 2023; Devault 1991; Sarkisian and Gerstel 2012). Thus, unequal distributions of emotional labor at work may be further exacerbated by unequal caring and emotion management at home. In both settings, women may perform an exhausting array of services that go unseen and unrewarded.

Race

Gender is one factor that can cause some workers to do extra emotional labor. Race is another. Despite the progress made since the civil rights movement, assumptions about race and ethnicity still shape Americans' perceptions and behavior (Feagin 2010). Thus, it seems likely that race can significantly affect the amount and kinds of emotion management that they must perform as they interact with customers, co-workers, and employers.

According to Wingfield (2010), there are at least two ways that emotional labor can be racialized rather than neutral. First, *workers may sometimes be held to different emotional standards*. For example, a white worker may be allowed a generous exception to the norm against expressing frustration in the workplace, whereas another employee may risk being viewed as an "angry black dude" or a "thug" (see also Jackson 2018). The same emotional display can be interpreted in different ways. In the first instance, a worker's anger might be seen as an indication that he is reacting to a genuine grievance or is exhibiting a mixture of passion, sincerity, and confidence; in the second instance, the worker's anger may be seen as inappropriate, threatening, and unprofessional.

In some settings, the norms governing emotional labor may be applied more even-handedly. However, that does not ensure equality, due to the fact that *racial prejudice may make conforming to norms much more difficult for some workers compared to others* (Wingfield 2010; 2021). Picture a black female worker who faces racism in the general society (e.g., being closely followed by security while shopping at stores). Then, imagine the same worker being exposed to racially offensive behavior in the workplace (e.g., a co-worker makes an insulting comment about "having soul food for lunch"). A worker of color may find obeying the norm "Be pleasant and limit anger" more challenging than a white worker would.

It's true that all workers face an array of stressors in their lives. However, it seems likely that racism can take an especially heavy toll. Imagine you are a person of color who works as a waiter or as a flight attendant. If some customers subtly (and not-so-subtly) treat you with less respect, then you may need to put more effort into suppressing your irritation and making customers happy. For example, Evans (2013) describes a case where a white passenger refused to be served drinks by a black flight attendant. Such blatant prejudice can generate intense emotions in an attendant, who may need to work hard to suppress negative feelings during and long-after a shift. The same is true of higher-level occupations, such as college professors and pilots. Harlow (2003) found that black professors were much more likely than white professors to report having students who questioned their authority and acted disrespectfully in class. Evans (2013), in turn, provides numerous examples of pilots being discriminated against by passengers and co-workers who doubt African Americans' ability to captain an aircraft (based on skin color alone). Black pilots may encounter looks of dismay, doubt, or even hatred as they walk through a terminal and board a plane. These and other discriminatory interactions force them to perform more emotional labor than their white counterparts (see also Evans and Moore 2015). Cottingham et al. (2018) found something similar in their research on the field of nursing. Nurses of color had to deal with overt discrimination (e.g., use of the "n" word) as well as microaggressions where patients and co-workers were uncooperative or questioned their abilities.[5]

The growth of social media adds another challenge. People of color may find themselves having to respond to racism or educate others about racial injustice on Twitter, Facebook, and other platforms. These difficult interactions can require significant emotion management—of oneself and others. Most famously, in recent years some NFL players have commented about discrimination in the criminal justice system and faced backlash from segments of their fanbase (Williams et al. 2019). Tennis players also report having to cope with devastating racist remarks in their social media feeds.[6]

Status

Gender and race may be partly incorporated into a broader form of inequality—status. Status is a nebulous concept, but it is closely associated with the amount of "respect" or "importance" a person is granted by others. People with higher status tend to be those who have more prestige, power, or wealth. Women and persons of color tend to have less of these characteristics, but so do others. For example, a detective has lower status than the chief of police, even if both are white men. Similarly, a celebrity like Jennifer Lawrence occupies a higher status level than most ordinary white women.

Status matters because it too affects emotional labor, putting more demands on some workers compared to others. Those with higher status tend to be protected from harsh emotions, by organizational shields and by status shields. *Organizational shields* are those barriers that limit or filter contact with customers and clients. For example, if undesirable interaction can be delegated to a receptionist, an assistant, or another lower-level employee, then one's emotional labor may be reduced (see Goodrum and Stafford 2003). *Status shields* are more subtle. Hochschild (1983:172) coined this term to refer to the tendency for the thoughts and feelings of higher status people to be taken more seriously. If you have a strong status shield, then people are more careful about what they do around you, and they are more attentive to what you say and feel. A complaint or a suggestion made by a high-status person resembles a boulder thrown into a pond, making a big impact and causing ripples; the same comment made by a low status person may land like a pebble. People are more attentive, respond more positively, and are less resistant to those with higher status. Consequently, the amount and intensity of their emotion labor tends to be reduced.

Imagine how hospital patients and their relatives might interact with doctors as opposed to nurses. A nurse is more likely to be challenged or treated disrespectfully than the doctor is. Similarly, when parents interact with an elementary school teacher, they may express more impatience and disdain than they might dare with a college professor. The professor, in turn, might display much less deference to an adjunct instructor than to a department chair or a dean.[7] Ironically, sometimes customers say the most hurtful things to minimum-wage workers with the least amount of power to enact changes; then, when a manager appears, their demeanor may become more respectful or subdued.

Diverse sources of status can intersect in nuanced ways. For example, you might wonder who has the stronger status shield: the white male paralegal or the attorney who is his boss—a woman of color. There are often no easy answers. The outcome may depend on various attributes of the workers, the clients, the specific interaction, the organization, the larger society, and so on (Lively 2013).

In this discussion of inequality—as with all the chapters in this book—my intention is not to give you facts to memorize. Rather, my goal is to encourage you to use sociological concepts to explore the world around you. Like *emotion norms* and *emotion management*, the concept of *status shield* is an idea you can creatively "test out" to see if it helps you make sense of your own experiences and observations.

Does Emotional Labor Damage Workers?

What can happen when workers are required to perform intensive emotional labor? Are there negative consequences to "manufacturing" emotions hour after hour, day after day, month after month, year after year, as a part of one's livelihood?

Consider an analogy with physical labor. Those who lift heavy items for a living (e.g., construction workers, UPS package shippers) might enjoy some physical benefits: they may burn calories, build muscles, and become fit. However, they might also injure themselves, temporarily or permanently, such as with back pain or carpal tunnel syndrome. Similarly, emotion laborers may accrue positive and negative consequences from repeatedly manipulating their feelings. These outcomes may be short lived or long lasting.[8]

Potential Drawbacks to Performing Emotional Labor

One potentially detrimental consequence of emotional labor is *burnout* (Hochschild 1983:187). Imagine a worker who must manage her emotions intensively and repeatedly, in a job requiring frequent customer contact. After a series of long and difficult shifts—perhaps working as a flight attendant during the holiday season, as a hostess at a popular restaurant, as a counselor to the abused or mentally ill—she might become exhausted to the point of "numbness." Such a worker may arrive home to her family and lack the desire or ability to feel anything. Faking and making displays of cheerfulness, or other company-mandated emotions, may lead to "periods of emotional deadness" (Hochschild 1983:187). Again, this condition seems somewhat analogous to manual labor, where workers may leave their jobs with a desperate need to rest their depleted and aching muscles or with a diminished ability to smell or hear. However, in the case of emotional labor, the "organ" that needs resting or becomes damaged is the capacity to feel—an ability that is essential to navigating one's relationships inside and outside the workplace.

A second negative consequence that may result from emotional labor is *ambivalence* or *confusion*. Hochschild (1983) argued that this is especially a risk for those workers who are trained and encouraged to use cognitive deep acting to produce more "genuine" emotional displays on the job. Flight attendants, for example, may be taught to view passengers as "mishandled" rather than obnoxious and as "house guests" rather than strangers. Or, a retail clerk may be socialized to think and act as though "The customer is never wrong." In either case, workers may struggle with conflicts between their own perspectives and those of their employer: *Am I thinking, acting, and feeling the way I am because that's what the company wants, or because I am being myself?* When employers meddle not only with display but with deeper emotional experiences, workers may struggle to identify and reconcile differences between their "work self" and their "true self" (Hochschild 1983:196–198).

Similarly, doctors may encounter some challenges reconciling their pre– and post-medical school perspectives (Smith and Kleinman 1989). During childhood, most of us are socialized to think of certain body parts as special or sacred. During medical training, however, students learn to redefine the human body in scientific and mechanical terms. Genitals and other aspects of the human body are given scientific names, broken down into their smallest components, and understood through their inner workings and anatomical connections. Doctors can employ the scientific perspective in order to suppress unwanted emotions on the job—such as disgust, nervousness, or sexual attraction. On the other hand, when they return home to their significant others, some students may have trouble viewing their romantic partners in the same way as they used to (Smith and Kleinman 1989:65–66).

Whereas ambivalence (or confusion) tends to result from cognitive deep acting, it is possible to experience negative impacts from doing surface acting as well. For example, some workers may feel dishonest when they are required to fake enthusiasm on a daily basis ("Welcome to our store! Thanks so much for coming! Have a great day!"). The repeated obligation to surface act may lead them to become *cynical* (see Hochschild 1983:135). They may view their occupation, or even themselves, more negatively over time: "This job is a scam and I am paid to fool people." Clearly, people's self-esteem and mental health might suffer if they think they are being duplicitous in service of an immoral or ignoble occupation.

Potential Benefits of Doing Emotional Labor

On some occasions, manual labor might lead to improved health, strength, or dexterity. Similarly, emotional laborers may develop abilities or skills—*emotional capital*—that they can use on and off the job (Ward and McMurray 2016:105). Some individuals' "people skills" may be improved as they learn how to manage emotions at work (Schweingruber and Berns 2005). An increased adeptness at surface and deep acting can help one navigate relationships with friends, relatives, neighbors, and teachers, as well as with customers, co-workers, and employers. For example, doctors and nurses may sometimes find it helpful to employ a scientific perspective on the human body, when relatives initiate (or avoid) difficult conversations about death or sexuality (Smith and Kleinman 1989).

Arguably, emotional labor can be beneficial by making one's workplace a more enjoyable setting. If one's co-workers actively foster positive attitudes in themselves and others, then that may make it easier for you to do the same. Imagine a waiter who needs to portray enthusiasm and happiness to customers—even performing an occasional birthday song with cheer. At the end of a shift, the worker might feel burned out, ambivalent, or cynical. On the other hand, the worker may feel "pumped up" and energized (Hallett 2003). For some people, a quiet shift might be less desirable than a loud and energetic shift that requires more surface and deep acting.

Emotional labor, like other forms of labor, can certainly be distasteful, oppressive, and alienating. On the other hand, it also has the potential to be meaningful and rewarding (Lopez 2006; Rodriquez 2011). Counselors, elementary school teachers, and nurses may perform repeated and intense emotion management as part of their jobs. However, at the end of a day, a year, or a career, they might reflect with pride on all the good that has resulted from their work. Surface and deep acting can lead to successful outcomes for others and for oneself. Imagine an alternative: a counselor or nurse who blatantly tells patients "You annoy me" or a teacher who occasionally mutters "You're a spoiled brat and I don't like you very much." Such "venting" may ultimately have negative effects on all parties involved, despite any momentary catharsis the worker may experience.

What Factors Make Emotional Labor Less Arduous?

Emotional labor can be exhausting and debilitating, or it can be enjoyable and rewarding. Much depends on the behavior of customers, who may have only a fleeting relationship with workers and can often be as cantankerous as they wish. However, much also depends on the characteristics and efforts of workers, employers, and occupational settings. In addition to inequalities of gender, race, and status, what kinds of factors determine whether emotional laborers will have positive or negative experiences? There are many possible answers to this question.

Whether due to nature or nurture, people's personalities may give them a greater *affinity* for particular jobs (Hochschild 2013). An extrovert may find it easier to surface and deep act through a long shift of waiting tables than an introvert might. A jovial person may be well-equipped to sell houses in a relaxed and lighthearted fashion but less able to do the surface and deep acting required to serve as a drill instructor for the military. Someone who grew up on a farm, raising and selling animals to market, may find it easier to perform euthanasia in veterinary school and afterward. Similarly, individuals who "lived, played, and/or worked in and around funeral homes" may be accustomed to thinking and talking about human death and thus be better equipped for a degree and career in mortuary science (Cahill 1999:111). One's proclivities—whether in-born or cultivated—can serve as *emotional capital* that individuals can strategically deploy in school and in an occupation, making them better equipped to perform the necessary emotion management (see also Mesquita and Delvaux 2013; Ward and McMurray 2016).

Closely related to affinity is the degree to which people feel personally invested or committed to a particular job (Tracy 2005). Sometimes workers see their occupations as a temporary-means-to-an-end. A fast-food position might be considered a stop-gap source of income while one goes to school or looks for something else. On other occasions, workers interpret their jobs more positively—less a "necessary evil" and more of a prized opportunity, if not one's "calling" in life (Lois and Gregson 2019). An occupation may be seen as an excellent stepping stone or as a highly valued destination in and of itself, regardless of pay. Thus, one's attitude towards a job might increase or decrease one's motivation to perform emotional labor. The lower a worker's opinion of a job, the more likely emotion management may be experienced as burdensome.

Our opinions of our occupations are not created willy-nilly, of course. Through socialization, we learn to give positive and negative meanings to particular occupations. The position of firefighter has been defined as heroic, especially since the 9/11 terrorist attacks (Monahan 2010). Also since 2001, the role of flight attendant has an increased emphasis on ensuring safety and security, which gives those workers more prestige and power (Santin and Kelly 2017). Other jobs—such as prison guards, sex workers, and garbage collectors—arguably provide important services yet are held in lower regard. Given the contentious and polarized state of American politics, some occupations have been recently demeaned, such as law enforcement officers. In the past few years politicians, pundits, activists, and others have criticized and called for the defunding of local police departments as well as of federal agencies like the Federal Bureau of Investigation and the Department of Justice.[9] Some border patrol agents say their job is "thankless" since they have been criticized from both sides of the political spectrum—for not doing enough to stop immigration and for being overaggressive and harsh (Rivera 2015). For any occupation, it may be easier to perform emotion management when one is engaged in an occupation consistently held in high esteem, both personally and socially.

Even if the pay is not very high, a person might collect "moral wages" from an occupation. In exchange for emotional labor, one may receive "the positive feelings and sense of satisfaction that come from seeing oneself as a caring and compassionate person who helps others in need" (Kolb 2014b:25). Some occupations entail a greater sense or interpretation that one is "doing good." Victim advocates, doctors, salespeople, and many others may (to various degrees) define their jobs in this manner, which serves as a buoyant or incentive for emotional laborers (Kolb 2014b; Schweingruber and Berns 2005; Smith and Kleinman 1989). Thus, the more one's job provides a valued identity and sense of moral purpose, the easier (or at least temporarily tolerable) one's surface and deep acting may be. As a professor, it is easier for me to surface and deep act my way through difficult interactions (such as disputes over grades) than it was for me when I held a tedious summer job serving customers at a swimming pool store. I am much more personally invested in my academic career; my current position is held in higher social esteem; and I am more inclined to believe that I am "doing good."

The status of one's customers or clients also shapes the difficulty of emotional labor. College students are relatively well-regarded—they are applauded for pursuing an education, for improving their financial prospects, and for becoming productive members of society. Compare them to lower-status clientele, such as convicted felons. A corrections officer may be instructed to treat inmates politely and with respect; however, when one is serving individuals who are defined as immoral savages, that may be difficult (Tracy 2005). Prison guards may have more difficulty performing the necessary surface and deep acting because their clientele is held in low regard, by society if not by the guards themselves.

The perceived success rate of one's occupation might also have a dramatic effect on emotional labor (Tracy 2005). If customers are almost always thrilled with a company's food, product, or service, then workers may find it relatively easy to work up enthusiastic displays of happiness. On the other hand, the opposite may also occur. Sometimes workers may come to believe that their customers rarely like the food; their students don't learn very much; their passengers usually arrive late and disappointed. In those situations, emotion management may be more likely to lead to burnout, ambivalence, or (especially) cynicism.

Employers, of course, might choose to take action to reduce the negative consequences of emotional labor. An important first step would be to simply acknowledge the existence of such labor. A worker is not likely to be appreciated or compensated for a task that escapes notice. Employers might provide occasional respites from performing emotional labor; employees might be encouraged to use a staff lounge to "vent" or complain, to make jokes, or to discuss coping strategies[10] (Tracy 2005); allowing eligible employees to work remotely for a portion of the week could also give them a break from doing face-to-face emotion management. Particularly enlightened employers might consider sharing power with employees or giving them more autonomy and flexibility (Ashkanasy and Daus 2002). The negative impact of emotional labor might be drastically reduced if workers had more "say" or control over the conditions of their job, such as the way they are trained, monitored, evaluated, and rewarded (Hochschild 1983:187).

What's the Point of this Chapter?

A student of mine composed an interesting essay about emotional labor after reading an earlier edition of this book. Their reflections are helpful even if not quite accurate. They wrote: "This chapter indicates that it is best to always let the customer be right, and to make sure that you listen to what they are saying or asking. Even if the customer is wrong, or there is an urge to argue back, good emotional labor training teaches employees to remain calm and polite." That's an understandable position to take, and it's a point of view that could be useful in many situations. Certainly, many employers would be thrilled to see a worker embrace that assumption. However, I'd say that's not really the point of this chapter.

I am attempting to expose you to concepts useful for making sense of the world and your place within it. After you learn and practice this book's vocabulary, you might then make a number of different arguments and use the ideas for many different purposes. You might garner or develop strategies for performing emotional labor more "professionally," as my student recommends. But you might also use the ideas to question authority. This chapter should empower you to ask fundamental questions—such as "Why do things this way?" and "What are the alternatives and the consequences?"—regarding the emotion norms, hiring, training, monitoring, sanctioning, and advertising that employers endorse. Each section of this chapter provides ideas that can be used to think critically about how emotional labor is organized and conducted, how things could be different, and who might suffer or benefit the most under current practices.

Almost no sociologist would simply embrace the expression "always let the customer be right." The flaws in that slogan are easily revealed by extreme incidents, such as when flight attendants are not only verbally abused but physically assaulted by unruly passengers.[11] Some customers may be simply and undeniably wrong, and may need to be told that, bluntly. But even more mundane aspects of emotional labor can be scrutinized and questioned, with an eye towards promoting greater equality and well-being rather than maximizing efficiency and profit.

Sociologists don't all think alike. However, most of them tend to be more interested in inequality (explaining and reducing it) rather than in making workers more effective. The type of research question they'll ask is less "How can we get workers to do 'good emotional labor' for employers and customers?" and more along the lines of "Who benefits and who is at risk when emotion management is required and tightly controlled by employers?"

Most of the sociologists I've cited in this chapter lean towards that social justice perspective as they simultaneously pursue the more basic goal of coining concepts and collecting data useful for understanding the social dimensions of emotions. However, you are free to use the ideas in this book any way you'd like, hopefully for your own personal benefit as well as the benefit of others. In Chapter 7 I say more about potential uses that the sociology of emotions might have for you.

Exercises

1 Describe the emotional labor that you perform in your current job (or that you imagine you will conduct in a future job). What kinds of positive and negative emotions tend to be generated by your occupation? What emotion norms govern your behavior? What kinds of surface and deep-acting strategies do you use in order to manage your own emotions as well as those customers, co-workers, and/or employers? Does this work have positive or negative effects on you? What conditions increase or decrease the burden of performing your emotional labor?
2 Find at least one person currently doing an occupation that you aspire to have in the future. Politely request an "informational interview" with that person. Ask about his or her daily routines and interactions with others. Guide the conversation towards the topic of emotional labor. Try to find out what kinds of surface and deep acting the person needs to do in order to manage their own emotions and those of clients, co-workers, or employers. You should probably submit a tentative list of interview questions to your instructor, and obtain their feedback and permission, before undertaking this exercise.
3 Google the customer service slogans I listed in the "Training" section of this chapter. Can you find them in the literature of specific companies? Can you find additional examples of slogans (and other tactics) that employers use to guide employees towards preferred deep acting strategies and emotions?
4 The next-to-last section of this chapter described several factors that may affect the degree to which emotional labor is burdensome or damaging. Can you think of some other potentially important factors to add to this list, based on your personal experiences, your observations of others, or your reading of the materials suggested below?

Notes

1 In this chapter, I have defined emotional labor somewhat broadly. Readers should note that—as with virtually all concepts (Harris 2022, ch. 3)—"emotional labor" can be conceptualized in many different ways. For example, some scholars' definitions emphasize deep acting rather than surface acting, or focus on customer service jobs over other occupations (see Grandey, Diefendorff, and Rupp 2013, ch. 1).

2 Here's a personal example: When I was an undergraduate at UC San Diego, I applied for a summer job as a resort worker in Guam. About halfway through my interview, the campus recruiter purposefully insulted me, asking a rude question about a particular line on my resume. Later I learned that she was trying to determine how I might react when confronted with a disrespectful customer.
3 Of course, another option is to replace human beings with artificial intelligence and other automated processes. For example, chatbots can be designed to appear happy or supportive, no matter how many hours they work or how many challenging customers they deal with on any given day.
4 *The Boston Globe* summarized occupational segregation in an interesting collection of graphics, available here: www.bostonglobe.com/metro/2017/03/06/chart-the-percentage-women-and-men-each-profession/GBX22YsWl0XaeHghwXfE4H/story.html (downloaded August 9, 2023). For example, in 2016, women accounted for more than 90 percent of preschool and kindergarten teachers, secretaries and administrative assistants, childcare workers, and nurses, and less than 10 percent of construction workers, truck drivers, aircraft pilots, and mechanics. Or, for an interactive tool based on 2019 Census data, see www.americanprogress.org/article/occupational-segregation-in-america/#interactive-visualization (downloaded August 9, 2023).
5 Readers interested in this topic may consider reading Kang (2003), who examines the intersection of race, class, gender, and feeling rules in the performance of body labor (e.g., manicures, massages).
6 For example, see this news story in Reuters (downloaded July 10, 2023): www.reuters.com/sports/tennis/racist-abuse-players-is-getting-worse-says-stephens-2023-05-29/
7 For a thorough examination of the emotional dynamics of academia, see Bloch (2012).
8 See also Wharton's (2009) review of the literature on this topic.
9 For examples of reporting on this, see www.washingtonpost.com/politics/2023/04/05/trump-defund-fbi-justice-department/ (downloaded July 19, 2023) and www.theguardian.com/us-news/2021/mar/07/us-cities-defund-police-transferring-money-community (downloaded August 9, 2023).
10 These strategies are not guaranteed to make emotional labor less arduous. For example, listening to a co-worker's traumatic story might transfer negative feelings from one person to another—spreading rather than reducing them (Groggel 2023).
11 See for example, reports of assaults on Frontier Airlines and American Airlines: www.cbsnews.com/colorado/news/assault-frontier-airlines-flight-attendant-denver-international-airport/
www.cnn.com/travel/article/unruly-passenger-flight-attendant-assault-american-airlines/index.html (downloaded July 10, 2023).

Suggested Readings

There are scores of fascinating case studies of emotional labor to choose from, on occupations as diverse as casino card dealers (Sallaz 2002), crime victim advocates and counselors, (Kolb 2011), detectives (Stenross and Kleinman 1989), exotic dancers (Deshotels and Forsyth 2006), firefighters (Scott and Myers 2005), insurance agents (Leidner 1993, ch. 4), litigators and paralegals (Pierce 1995), models (Mears and Finley 2005), prison guards (Tracy 2005), public relations practitioners (Yeomans

2019), river guides (Holyfield and Jonas 2003), and staff at abortion clinics and animal shelters (Arluke 1998; Wolkomir and Powers 2007), just to name a few possibilities. Readers might enter "emotional labor" and "[insert a type of occupation here]" into www.scholar.google.com or the database *Sociological Abstracts* (available at many university libraries), to see if they can find any research that fits their interests. Virtually all research on emotional labor has been inspired or at least informed by Hochschild's (1983) study of flight attendants and bill collectors, so her book is of course a valuable resource.

Although many useful state-of-the-field overviews have been written as individual chapters or articles (Lively 2006; Meanwell, Wolfe, and Hallett 2008; Wharton 2009), the following edited collection provides an outstanding discussion:

Grandey, Alicia A., James M. Diefendorff, and Deborah E. Rupp (editors). 2013. *Emotional Labor in the 21st Century: Diverse Perspectives on Emotion Regulation at Work*. New York: Routledge.

6 Identifying Emotions

How do you feel? This commonplace question is asked in a wide range of circumstances. Sometimes "feel" refers to one's state of health—as when a friend inquires whether we are getting over the flu. On other occasions, people may intend this question to be an inquiry about our emotions. Are you happy? Upset? In love? Angry? In those circumstances, every time we answer we are engaging in the process of *labeling emotions*—the topic of this chapter.

From a strictly biological point of view, it makes little difference what we call our emotions. If we stumble across a bear while hiking through the woods, we are likely to experience a widening of the eyes, a rapid heart rate, and increased adrenaline. We're "afraid." Physiologically, we may experience "fear," regardless of whether we use that term to think and talk about it. Examples such as these can be used to portray emotions as genetically hard-wired responses to environmental stimuli.

From a sociological perspective, however, it matters greatly whether and how we label feelings—both during the event and afterwards. Thinking "I'm so scared right now!" might amplify one's fear, whereas telling yourself "You're fine—stay calm and don't run" might help suppress the feeling, as a form of deep acting. Moreover, the-story-of-the-dramatic-bear-encounter might be retold dozens of times, in conversation with others. In those circumstances, it may make a significant difference whether narrators describe themselves as "terrified," "a little bit concerned," or "not scared in the least." Depending on the context, some descriptions might be deemed humorous, brave, or foolish, and thus shape how others think about and act towards us.

Before we examine the social processes involved in labeling feelings, let's give some more attention to the physiology of emotions. A greater appreciation of the ambiguity of our bodily sensations opens up space for our subsequent discussions of emotional identification as a cultural, interpretive, and interactive process.

DOI: 10.4324/b23334-6

Bodily Ambiguity

It is tempting to argue that everyone is an "expert" on their own bodies and feelings. After all, we live *in* and *with* our physical selves every day. So, from a common-sense perspective, identifying feelings may seem like a simple matter. "I know when I am jealous, angry, or sad," you might be thinking. What could be difficult about labeling one's feelings? However, if you are willing to consider the topic a little more carefully, perhaps you will find that naming your emotions is more complicated, nuanced, and fascinating than you realized. Let's start by examining four reasons why it can be difficult to rely on bodily sensations when identifying feelings.[1]

Earlier I described an increased heart rate and elevated adrenaline as indicators of fear. That seems reasonable. However, the problem is that those sensations might be linked to a variety of emotions, such as pleasurable excitement (e.g., "Guess what—you won the lottery!") or anger ("Some jerk keyed my car!"). Thus, the first reason identifying emotions can be difficult is that different emotions can have similar physiological manifestations.

The sensations accompanying emotions are not clear cut or easily distinguished (Rosenberg 1990; Schachter and Singer 1962). If our bodies provided unequivocal information about our emotions, then identifying them might be a simpler matter. That's not the case. Individuals need to interpret the meaning of their own (and others') reactions. For example, crying can be a sign of happiness, fear, and other emotions besides sadness.[2] I remember crying when I tried the sport of boxing for the first time, as an eight-year-old. A neighborhood friend invited me to test it out in his parents' garage. In less than a minute our casual sparring escalated until eventually I was punched in the face and burst into tears. When my friend asked me "What's wrong?" I did not have a good answer. I was not in a great deal of pain, nor was I sad. All I could say was that "I don't think I like boxing!"

People may live with their bodies every day, but they don't systematically study physiology, like some researchers do. Thus, you might wonder: Can scientists link different emotions to specific physiological manifestations? Psychologists find this to be an impossible task (Barrett 2006). So, what is complicated in the lab may be even more complicated for laypersons in their everyday lives. As we go about our busy days, we can't simply look to our bodies for obvious telltale signs of what we're feeling.

A second reason identifying emotions may be difficult is that feelings may not come one at a time. On many occasions, we may experience multiple feelings simultaneously (Rosenberg 1990). When we ride a roller coaster, for example, we may feel fear along with pleasurable excitement. (And, if you are like my spouse, mix in a bit of irritation directed towards the person who convinced you to take the ride.) Similarly, at a horror movie, audience members may feel afraid while enjoying themselves. One of my students told me that the act of giving birth filled her with joy and fear, along with aching pain.

Or, consider a different familial example. When a parent dies, sadness may be the expected emotion. However, if the deceased had been suffering from dementia for years, then the bereaved may feel relief (as well as guilt over feeling relief) at the same time as sadness (Holstein and Gubrium 1995:35). Or, if a parent were to pass away while undergoing a relatively routine medical procedure, one's sadness may be complicated by feelings of anger towards the hospital staff.

Likewise, the discovery of a cheating fiancé may generate feelings of anger, embarrassment, betrayal, and disappointment. Even if there were distinct physiological sensations connected to each of these emotions—a big assumption indeed—the sensations might be jumbled together and difficult to disentangle.

A third reason that identifying emotions may be difficult is that human beings lack a precise system for measuring them (Rosenberg 1990). We can dispense sugar by the teaspoon, tablespoon, or cup, but there is no similar system for gauging the happiness or love we experience or express. Despite the once-popular "mood rings," we do not possess emotional thermometers that clearly indicate just how angry we are. Nor is there currently "an app for that." In many everyday situations, people claim that they (or their companions) are "full of" pride, love, or resentment. Song lyrics also express these ideas. In "Work Song," Irish musician Hozier suggests his romantic partner made him "so full of love I could barely eat" whereas Billie Holiday sang long ago that she was "filled with despair … in my solitude." Other artists sing about emotions being depleted, especially being "out of love" (Google that phrase plus the band Air Supply, hip hop artist Shad, or popstar Alessia Cara). These notions—that we can be "full of" or "out of" an emotion—can prompt images of a gasoline gauge in an automobile.[3] Unlike our cars, however, we do not come equipped with dashboard indicators that tell us how much of a feeling we possess. Nor can we insert a dipstick to measure how much anger we have accumulated, like checking the oil level in an engine.

People do "read the tea leaves" or make use of indeterminate bodily signs as best they can. For example, we might tell people who are "red in the face" that they seem angry. We can't easily prove it, however. They can choose to reject the label and claim to feel frustration, exasperation, or passion instead—or they might argue that their face becomes bright red whenever they exercise, drink alcohol, or are too warm. Perhaps scientists may someday develop a foolproof system for determining the truth of what we feel, by systematically examining facial expressions. But for today, in everyday life, there's no simple measurement device for conclusively settling the debate. Rather, our physiology and behavior must be interpreted as we assign labels to ourselves and to others.

There is a fourth reason why bodily ambiguity may not facilitate emotional identification, which can be stated simply: Some emotions may not be accompanied by much physiological arousal at all. Not all emotions are felt as strongly as panic, outrage, or euphoria. There might not be very much "going on" in our bodies when we experience admiration, affection, contentment, gratitude, hope, nostalgia, or pride (Averill 1974:176; Harré 1992). Once again, our bodies cannot always be relied upon to simply tell us what we are feeling, since some feelings may be more easily "noticed" or "recognized" than others. This too provides further cause to move away from physiology and towards social factors, in our examination of emotional identification.

Social Factors that Guide Emotional Identification

It's helpful to begin a discussion of emotional identification by highlighting physiological ambiguity: it shows that there must be more to the process than a quick consultation with our bodies. However, there is a risk. Just because I discussed this topic first, let's *not* assume that our bodies are always central to the process of labeling feelings. Quite the contrary. On many occasions, the body may play a very minor role in emotional identification (Pollak and Thoits 1989:25). There are many social factors that may have a much greater effect on the labeling process. Let's examine seven of them.

1) Vocabularies of Emotion

Because we have discrete words for emotions—jealousy, love, panic, shame—people often assume that these terms refer to clear-cut entities. We forget that our categories are merely *tools* that people created in an attempt to make sense out of things. It's important to remind ourselves that language is an artificial, human creation.

Cross-cultural comparisons can help us recognize the arbitrariness of language. When it comes to emotions, not all cultures have developed the same conceptual resources. This can be seen in the number of terms for emotion that different languages possess. For example, some scholars estimate that the Chewong (a small group in Southeast Asia) use only eight emotion words, whereas the Taiwanese use over 700 (Clark 2002:166; Heelas 1986:238). Wallace and Carson (1973:5) searched through Webster's *New Collegiate Dictionary* and the *Dictionary of American Slang* and found over 2,000 English emotion terms. (However, keep in mind there is no perfect way to define what counts as an "emotion word" or collect instances of them.)

Sometimes words seem relatively easy to translate from one language to another, such as "amor" for "love." Other times, translation takes a bit more effort. Germans, for example, have ready access to the term "Schadenfreude," which refers to feeling pleasure at the misfortune of others. South Asian Buddhists can invoke "mudita" to describe the opposite: joy at the fortune of others (Casioppo 2020). The Ifaluk, who live on a Micronesian atoll, use the term "fago" to express a complex mixture of love, compassion, and sadness (Lutz 1988). The Japanese invoke "amae" to reference the "positive feeling of basking in one's complete dependence on another" (Clark 2002:166; see also Goddard 2002). Arguably, these convenient options are missing in English.

If we don't lack a term entirely, there are at least times we must make do with cruder tools. The Ifaluk, for example, differentiate between two types of disgust—moral and physical. English speakers, in contrast, make the same word do double duty: we describe our responses to despicable behavior and to the smell of spoiled milk as "disgust." Arguably, our vocabulary is cruder or less specific in this case. In other areas, English seems more precise. For example, Americans usually distinguish between embarrassment, shame, guilt, and shyness, whereas the Javanese[4] use a single word—"isin"—to refer to all those feelings (Russell 1991). Some African languages describe sadness and anger using a single word, and the Illongot (in the Philippines) do the same when characterizing anger and envy (Heelas 1986:240). Thus, when individuals identify their emotions, they do so using the conceptual resources that their particular cultures happen to provide.

Vocabularies of emotion vary historically as well as cross-culturally. Even within my lifetime, I have seen the rise of three emotion categories. In the first twenty years of my life—the 1970s and 1980s—I don't think I heard anybody use the concept of *road rage* to make sense out of a driver's behavior. Nor did my friends speak of their need to feel *closure* after a break-up, a death, or the end of a semester. And no one yelled *schwing* to indicate feelings of lust or sexual attraction. All these concepts were popularized in the 1990s.[5] Just because a new category of emotion is created doesn't mean it will thrive, however. Use of *schwing* has declined dramatically and is being replaced by descriptions of lusty people as "thirsty" or "thirsting over [an attractive person]." Relatively few people now admit to melancholy, despite its ascendance in the Middle Ages (Harré and Finlay-Jones 1986). Some emotions become virtually extinct, which is what seems to have happened to *accidie*, a once-prominent feeling of "boredom, dejection or even disgust with fulfilling one's religious duty" (Harré and Finlay-Jones 1986:221).

Even the word "emotion" is itself only around 500 years old, derived from the Latin verb "movere," which meant to move, migrate, or transfer (Averill 1974; Franks 1994; see also Dixon 2012). The word *motion* is built right into the concept of emotion, which reveals its humble etymological beginnings.

With the invention of the internet, emotional identification has been shaped by conventions that pervade emailing, texting, and tweeting. Rather than describing myself verbally, I can copy/paste a GIF or type an emoticon—such as :-) or :-(—that represents how I feel. The creation and spread of such technology-driven symbols is, arguably, another historical development in the options that (some) people have for depicting their feelings (Derks et al. 2008; Stanton 2014). This chapter's **Spotlight on Research** explores how people use images to describe their own and others' emotions, by looking at Vyvyan Evans' (2017) work on emojis.

2) Metaphors

The vocabularies people use to describe their emotions can be quite creative. Instead of saying "I'm angry," people can describe themselves as fuming, smoldering, or red hot. All three descriptors are metaphors that draw analogies between anger and fire. If we compare the body to a container, then we can add these expressions as well:

- You make my blood boil
- Simmer down, dude
- I need to blow off steam
- Don't blow a gasket
- I flipped my lid
- Smoke is coming out of your ears
- I'm going to explode

(Kövecses 2000:148)

People are socialized into using metaphorical expressions to depict emotions. I would bet that most American readers have used some but not all of the above metaphors, depending on the linguistic preferences of their friends, family, and co-workers. Of course, individuals raised in another culture may be encouraged to use completely different emotion metaphors. The Japanese frequently locate anger in the belly; speakers of Zulu lack the expression "blowing off steam," but they do speak of "blowing a gale" (Kövecses 2000:170–171).

I don't want to give you the impression that there is no consistency in how different cultures use metaphors to describe emotions. Cross-cultural overlaps and patterns can be found (see also Wierzbicka 1999). These may be tied to human physiology, to recurring environmental patterns, or to other factors that diverse cultures share in common. Certain tendencies may make some descriptions more likely than others. For example, anger tends to coincide with an increase in body temperature, which perhaps partly explains why heat metaphors for the emotion can be found in various languages, such as English, Japanese, Hungarian, and Chinese (Kövecses 2000:158). Similarly, the experience of lust shares some behavioral parallels with the experience of hunger. Put bluntly, people may

- Feel hungry, look for food, get some, feel satisfied
- Feel horny, look for sex, get some, feel satisfied

Given these loose parallels, it's perhaps not surprising that different cultures have developed food metaphors to characterize their sexual "appetites." Speakers of Chagga[6] refer to partners who taste good, just as English speakers sometimes say a person looks good enough to eat (Emanatian 1995). However, differences still can be found. In Chagga, only male lust is characterized as hunger, whereas both men and women can be described as "sex starved"[7] by

English speakers. Thus, individuals' vocabularies of emotion can be shaped by their culture's language as well as its specific norms about gender.

Metaphors of emotion are so common that we take them for granted. Earlier in this book (Chapter 3), I used the terms "down" and "low" as synonyms for "sad." Most readers probably did not think much about my use of those terms. Many of us tend simply to assume "happiness is up" and "sadness is down" (Lakoff and Johnson 1980:15). Perhaps this is because sadness as well as sickness may be associated with a drooping posture or with lying down. Even plants tend to wilt or collapse when they are "not doing well," so perhaps it's no surprise that "down" is used to describe negative feelings. However— surprising or not—these metaphorical expressions are cultural conventions that shape the ways that people identify their emotions.

3) Emotion Labels as Perspectives on Situations

So far I've argued that emotional identification is shaped by the vocabularies (including metaphors) that cultures create and encourage their members to use. Even if emotions are rooted in biology, our descriptions of them are irrevocably tied to social norms and customs.

In this section, I will outline a third social dimension of emotional identification: The words we use to label emotions may be oriented more to our thoughts about situations than to our thoughts about our bodies (Hochschild 1983, Appendix B).

If bodily sensations were essential to the way we label our emotions, then our categories would reflect that. However, it's hard to think of an emotion that is named after a physiological state (Hochschild 1983:223). We tend not to say "I feel adrenaline about that." We might tell others that we felt "butterflies" in our stomachs or that we were "shivering," but those kinds of terms usually provide context or support to a more specific emotion label, such as stage fright or romantic love.

Instead, *the terms we use to characterize emotions can be seen as descriptions of our perspectives*. If I were to ask how you felt about performing in a school play, you would likely discuss the audience ("It's a small and friendly crowd, so I'm not too *worried* "), the probability of things going awry ("I'm *afraid* I'll forget my lines!"), or the risk to your reputation ("If I screw up I'll be so *embarrassed*!"). All these statements seem oriented to one's perspective on the situation more than to one's bodily state. The emotion category provides a shorthand summary of our thoughts. "I'm *nervous* about tonight's show." Why? "Because X, Y, and Z may go wrong." An actor may or may not experience heightened bodily arousal as a performance approaches, but those sensations seem secondary. The choice of labels is more directly tied to one's assessment of the situation, which is shaped by the importance the person places on the theater, on their reputation, on the perceived likelihood of success, and on other factors that are matters of culture and perspective, not physiology.

Earlier in this chapter I referred to the death of a parent as a situation where emotions—and physiological sensations—can be mixed. Another way to frame this example is to say that one's *attention* is mixed (Hochschild 1983:224). When focusing on never seeing a parent again, I may describe my feelings as sadness. When considering that death has brought an end to a parent's pain and suffering, I may say I feel relief. When focusing on the unnatural cause of the death (e.g., a medical mistake or a drunk-driving accident), I may describe what I'm feeling as anger.

In all these cases, the emotion category seems chosen to reflect or encapsulate one's changing perspective on the situation more than to describe changes in one's physiology.

Imagine what you will say when someone asks you "How does it feel to be graduating from college?" Perhaps you will say you are *sad* to say goodbye to friends; *excited* to face new challenges; *anxious* about the job market; or just *glad* to be done with final exams. Do you think your bodily state will play a lead or supporting role as you identify your feelings? I would guess that you will select labels that reflect your cognitive appraisal of the situation much more than your appraisal of your physiology.

4) Emotional Identification as Impression Management

The process of emotional identification is still far more social than we've yet discussed. Yes, our bodies are ambiguous. True, we rely on culturally created vocabularies to label feelings. And, these labels are linked more to our perspectives on situations than to bodily changes. But often *the interactional context* of labeling is the key factor in identifying what we "feel." Individuals may look outward to the setting, rather than inward to their bodies (or even to their cognitive perspectives), when labeling feelings. Descriptions of emotions can be used "rhetorically"—that is, to shape how people think and feel about us (Coupland et al. 2008; Edwards 1999; Harré 1992; Wilkins 2008).

For example, it is commonplace for people to begin a public address by saying they are "very happy to be here." When this labeling occurs, it seems unlikely that the speaker has done a careful examination of his or her physiology in order to measure the degree to which any emotions are present: "After consulting my viscera, I've determined I'm only feeling happiness—and a lot of it." Rather, the speaker is probably—at least on many occasions—concerned far less with bodily sensations (or even with reporting their cognitive assessment of the situation) and much more about making a good impression on the audience.

Speakers would risk making a bad impression if they began by saying "I'm bored to be here." Even a positive but lukewarm emotion—"I'm mildly content to be here"—might be seen as strange or downright offensive to some audiences. Thus, even though these descriptions might be honest, speakers may be judged harshly for admitting them.

Imagine what would happen if a presenter felt mixed emotions, and explained each feeling at the beginning of a speech:

> Before I start, let me say that I am very excited and happy to be here. I have some interesting material to share with you, and I look forward to hearing your feedback. I am also nervous since I am worried about making a mistake and looking foolish. In addition, I am a little annoyed about the height of the podium, which is not ideal. Furthermore, my marriage is going through a rough patch, so I am carrying around some residual sadness from that.

Such an opening statement may be possible but seems highly improbable. Rather, when people label their feelings at the beginning of a speech, it seems likely that they will provide a *selective and context-sensitive depiction* rather than a comprehensive and objective account of their emotions. Despite the proverb "Honesty is the best policy," in practice people find that their thoughts and feelings frequently need to be hidden, disguised, downplayed, or exaggerated. We control this information in order to save face, protect relationships, avoid conflict, and otherwise guide interaction in desired directions (Turner, Edgley, and Olmstead 1975).

What is true of public speeches is true of other contexts. Imagine the simple question "How are you?" being asked of you in a variety of circumstances. When a friend asks you this question in the hallway between classes, you might give a different answer than if the conversation were happening in the privacy of your apartment. When the same question is asked by a parent over the phone, you might give a third type of response. And then if a counselor were to ask "How are you?" during a formal therapy session, you might provide a fourth account. "I'm doing fine" might suffice in the hallway but be too brief and impersonal elsewhere. A description of the lustful feelings one has for a classmate might fit perfectly during a private conversation with a friend, but not in the hallway between classes or on the phone with a parent. And a frank admission about having low self-esteem might be fully appropriate in a therapy session, but completely inappropriate for a quick hallway greeting. Picture this hypothetical interaction:

"Hi Suzanne! How ya doin'?"
"I'm questioning my self-worth today. How are you?"

The context, the audience, and our interactional goals all shape the way we describe our feelings (Harris and Ferris 2009). When talking to our companions, we may characterize our emotions in particular ways, in order to elicit desired reactions. For example, if a person doesn't want a parent to worry too much, then negative emotions might be purposefully excluded or downplayed: "I'm a little nervous about my math class." Earlier in the day, the same student might have said "I'm totally panicked about my math class!" in order to provoke sympathy and amusement in a friend.

It is possible for us to lie outright when we describe our feelings (Turner et al. 1975). People may be utterly cunning and manipulative when they tell an employer or instructor that they are too distraught (from a family tragedy) to do their work. The tragedy, or the sadness, may be complete fabrications.

On the other hand, the more interesting and (hopefully) more likely possibility is that people either exaggerate slightly or else focus on different things as they talk to different people in different contexts. For example, during the course of a day, a student may alternate between nervousness, panic, and indifference about a math class. Later, when asked "How are you doing?" the student can pick and choose which honest feeling to report. Or, if a moderate amount of nervousness is felt relatively consistently, then that emotion can be played up or played down, depending on the person's goal at the moment—eliciting sympathy, prompting amusement, calming a concerned parent, demonstrating competence, excusing behavior, and so on (see also Coupland et al. 2008; Locke 2003). Sometimes a person's goal is to "not be boring," which can motivate us to exaggerate a feeling to make it more dramatic. In our pursuit to make others like us, we may be tempted to report feelings that are extreme. Saying "I absolutely love Thai food!" makes us a more attractive dinner companion than the statement "Yes, I enjoy Thai food." And saying "My math test could be a challenge" is likely boring compared to claiming "I'm terrified of my math test!"

Careful readers should notice here a partial overlap between Chapters 3 and this one, Chapter 6. In Chapter 3, we discussed surface acting (managing how one appears to feel) as something accomplished through the manipulation of facial expressions, tone of voice, gestures, clothing, and wording. That last technique, wording, overlaps clearly with the process of emotional identification: we sometimes label our feelings strategically in order to influence how others perceive us. Nevertheless, Chapters 3 and 6 cover distinct topics. Much surface acting is done without explicitly labeling our emotions (e.g., we can pretend to be excited about a gift without saying "I love it"), and not all labeling can be reduced to surface acting (e.g., see some of the other sections here in Chapter 6).

5) Interpersonal Emotional Identification

The fifth social dimension in my list takes emotional labeling even further outside the person experiencing a feeling, by highlighting the participation of others in the process. Emotional identification is not the exclusive prerogative of isolated individuals. Like emotion management (Chapter 3), the labeling of feeling can be a group project. People often receive assistance—wanted or unwanted—when identifying their feelings.

Consider the concept of *interactional coaching* (Ferris and Harris 2011). In everyday conversations, people coach or guide us towards using particular emotional labels. One way they do this is by providing or endorsing potential options for us to use:

- Congratulations on graduating! I bet you are so *excited*!
- I'm sorry about your mom. You must be *devastated*.
- I heard what your ex did. I'm sure you're really *pissed off*, right?

Sometimes our interactional coaches provide two candidates or answers to choose from—as if we were voting or taking a multiple-choice exam:

- Are you *scared* or *eager* to be starting your new job?
- Are you *envious* of your friend's success, or are you *proud* of her?
- Were you *satisfied* with your grade or *upset* about it?

Of course, people can ask open-ended questions about our emotions. However, even a broad question such as "How do you feel about [X]?" constitutes coaching, as it encourages us to focus on and report about our experiences using a vocabulary of emotion rather than some other terminology. A much different response might be received if the question were phrased as "What are your thoughts on [X]?" or "How would you rate [X] on a scale of 1 to 10?"

The "help" that we receive from others does not end once we have selected a particular label for our emotions. People may encourage us to change our description to one that is weaker, stronger, or completely different. Interactional coaching thus goes hand in hand with another social process—the *upgrading* and *downgrading* of emotional labels (Staske 1996), which occurs when we replace an initial description with a stronger or weaker category.

For example, people often express their disapproval of others' behavior. Sometimes speakers go so far as to say the equivalent of "I hate President Biden!" or "I hate the MAGA movement!" Not all listeners will endorse or tolerate such harsh statements, however. People like to remind others that "hate" is an extreme or unacceptable emotion. "Be careful. Hate is a strong word," they may advise. In response, the speaker might quickly downgrade their putative emotion to a less intense label. "OK, fine. Let's just say I *dislike* them and leave it at that."

Similarly, our companions sometimes question our use of positive emotional categories. When one person says they "absolutely love Thai food," another might childishly tease "Do you want to marry it?" Such a question can be seen as a prompt to modify an initial description in a lower direction: "No, but I am quite fond of it," the speaker might reply—a significant reduction from "absolutely love."

In addition to encouraging us to downgrade an emotional category, our companions might coach us into the opposite direction, encouraging an upgrade to a more intense label. For example, I often say "Love you" to my spouse, during the course of routine interactions (e.g., cooking dinner). In response, she lightheartedly asks "Really? How much?" The big grin on her face shows me that she is not really doubting my sincerity but is gently prodding me to offer a bigger display (and an upgraded characterization) of my emotions. In response I might say "I love you THIS MUCH"—while holding my arms out wide, to intensify my description. "I love you more than life itself" would be another (sappy) option. A third choice is to say "I love you more than ice cream itself," which is a joke that works because she knows that's my favorite dessert.

There are times when people may guide us towards upgrading the descriptions of negative emotions, as well. For instance, people who are depressed may say they feel "fine" or "not too bad." In response, their companions may say "Are you sure? You seem really down" and encourage the use of a stronger, and perhaps more candid, label (Staske 1996). Again, my point is that labeling emotions is a social act, and that it can have consequences for how we see ourselves, for how others see us, and for subsequent interactions.

6) Debating "Who Knows Best" about Emotions

As we've discussed, people may collaborate with us as we apply labels to emotional experiences of ourselves and others. That collaboration can be relatively consensual, if people kindly coach us towards labels that we don't mind adopting. On the other hand, collaboration may be contentious. Emotional identification can be a group project, but one where people disagree on how best to characterize an emotional state (Gubrium 1989).

Disagreements can center not only on which label is correct, but on the grounds or warrants different people may have for knowing about emotions. Who is in the best position to say what a person is feeling? This simple question may be more difficult to answer than you realize.

In Chapter 1, I argued that Americans often assume emotions are private possessions. This leads to a strong sense of confidence that the individual who is experiencing an emotion can speak most authoritatively about it. People frequently claim that they have *privileged access* (Gubrium and Holstein 2009) to their own emotional states, and that others lack the ability to comprehend their feelings:

- Don't tell me what I feel! You don't know how it feels to be me.
- Unless you've suffered the hell of depression, then you can't understand what I'm going through.
- You don't have children, right? That means you have no idea how joyful or frustrating it can be to raise a teenager.

As compelling as these arguments may seem, they are not the only ones that are made. Privileged access is only one type of claim, and it may not win the day, despite the popular assumption that emotions are private possessions.

Interestingly, one kind of argument that undermines privileged access comes from the experiencing individuals themselves. Sometimes people argue that they lack the ability to understand their own feelings, in effect *disavowing privileged access* (cf. Gubrium and Holstein 1990):

- I don't know how I feel about that.
- I need to sort out my feelings.
- I thought I was in love, but now I think it was just infatuation.
- Before I read that poem, I didn't have the words to make sense of what I was feeling.

This scenario was presented in the classic song "I Can't Explain" by The Who in 1965. The singer appears to speak to a romantic partner with lines like "Got a feeling inside (can't explain). It's a certain kind (can't explain). I feel hot and cold (can't explain). Yeah, down in my soul (can't explain)." Fifty years later, rapper Lil Baby recorded a similarly titled song with the recurring line "Don't know how to feel, I got some feelings that I can't explain." Both sets of lyrics demonstrate *disclaiming privileged access*, which people do when they assert an inability to interpret or express their own emotions.

Even if an individual remains confident about their knowledge of their own emotional states, others can propose their own interpretations. At times, other people go so far as to claim that they know better what a particular individual is feeling, by *asserting the validity of an outsider's perspective* (cf. Gubrium and Holstein 1990):

- You say you love me, but actions speak louder than words, and your actions are telling me that you don't really care about me.
- Your face is red and your voice is raised. To me, that means you're angry, no matter what you say. You're not fooling me!
- You say you're just being cautious, but I think your fear of failure is keeping you from taking the necessary risks.
- I *do* know what you're feeling, because I went through a very similar situation last year and came out the other side of it.

Friends, relatives, and co-workers may challenge an individual's emotional self-knowledge, using nothing more than common-sense arguments. Another approach, however, is to invoke a technical or psychological diagnosis. Counselors, therapists, psychiatrists, and psychologists have developed a range of concepts that can be used—even by laypersons—to question individuals' claims about their own feelings (see Kalat and Shiota 2007:300). *Denial*, which occurs when individuals refuse to admit to themselves that they have a problem, is one such concept. People with "anger management issues" may be described as "in denial" if they complain that their companions are just overly sensitive. *Projection* is another option for discrediting someone's portrayal of their own emotional states. Projection is said to occur when individuals attribute their negative feelings to another person, rather than claim them as their own. For instance, a person may say "Javier hates me" rather than admitting that the dislike resides within him- or herself. So, an individual may be challenged to "Stop projecting and be honest about your feelings!" *Displacement* provides a third option. This phenomenon occurs when disturbing feelings are directed towards someone or something other than the source that provoked them. For example, a worker might yell at his spouse at home rather than express anger to customers or to his boss. Thus, a relative, counselor, or a friend might ask a man to consider whether he is *really* angry at his wife (despite his claims to the contrary), or if in fact he is simply "taking out" his frustrations on his spouse.

Spotlight on Research

Expressing Emotions Through Emojis

Much social interaction has moved online, and emotional identification along with it. The internet offers new contexts and methods for depicting feelings, not only with words but with images as well. Most readers of this book have probably composed a text, email, or tweet that portrays their emotional state by clicking on the images that come pre-programmed in your software—a heart, a thumbs up, a middle finger, a face that is smiling, frowning, or winking, and so on. These are *emojis*, a Japanese term that loosely translated means "picture-word" (Danesi 2017:11). *Emoticons*, in contrast, are created with characters found on a regular keyboard, such as using the colon-hyphen-parenthesis to make a smiley face :-).

Emojis have exploded in popularity since the advent of smart phones. Some commentators believe that emojis' widespread adoption is damaging people's ability to express themselves. The ability and inclination to craft a spontaneous sentence may diminish when we can click on a handy image and let it do the talking for us. Linguistics professor Vyvyan Evans (2017) disagrees with this pessimistic view. In his readable book, *The Emoji Code: The Linguistics Behind Smiley Faces and Scaredy Cats*, Evans argues that emojis enable effective communication rather than detract from it. By drawing on the concepts of *kinesics* and *paralinguistics*, Evans shows how emojis help provide the same kind of information in textually mediated interactions that nonverbal cues do in face-to-face interaction.

Kinesics refers to nonverbal bodily movements that help us communicate in daily life. Think of facial expressions, hand gestures, arm movements, eye contact, posture, and the like. *Paralinguistics* refers to the way we vocalize our words, such as our tone, volume, and rhythm, and whether we laugh or stutter as we speak.

In face-to-face interaction, kinesics and paralinguistics significantly shape the meaning of our words. If I say in monotone "That was delicious" after a meal, the compliment might be received as faint or insincere. If I say the food was "deeee-licious!"—extending the first syllable and giving it a higher pitch (paralinguistics) while smiling, nodding, and rubbing my belly (kinesics)—that would convey much more excitement and make a much different impact on the chef.

Building on prior work by anthropologists, Evans argues that there are several ways that kinesic and paralinguistic cues shape the meanings of our in-person verbal communications. Evans then explains that emojis perform the same functions for text-based communication online. Let's delve into a portion of his argument, focusing on examples related to emotion.

The first function is *substitution*: emojis can replace or substitute for words. A person could text "I'm mad at you" or they could choose to simply send a picture of an angry face—just as (in face-to-face interaction) they could choose to silently scowl rather than "using their words" to say how they feel. A second function of nonverbal cues is *reinforcement*. Emojis can be used to confirm or strengthen a verbal cue. Online, an individual might type "I'm excited to come to your party!" followed by a thumbs-up emoji, just as they might say those words and display that hand gesture in everyday life. The thumbs up reinforces the written or spoken statement. Alternatively, people can use nonverbal cues to purposefully *contradict* their linguistic messages, giving people "mixed messages," which is a third function. In face-to-face interaction, I might sarcastically say "Wooow, I'm sooo eager to attend" as I wink at you; similarly, in a text I might type the words "Can't wait" followed by an eye-rolling emoji or an upside-down happy face, or perhaps even a poop emoji. Here the emojis, just like the kinesic and paralinguistic cues, tell my audience that I mean something different than what I've stated verbally or in writing.

Digital textual communication occurs in a sort of vacuum, absent the physical signals of copresence. Without that context, "a rushed email, or a casual SMS can sound detached, snotty, or worse," leading us to be perceived as an "angry jerk" (Evans 2017:136). For Evans, smiley faces, winking faces, hearts, and other symbols can be used to convey a tone of friendliness or lightheartedness that prevents "miscommunication and offense."

With points like these in mind, Evans (2017:129) argues that emojis are crucial in online environments: "[The] Emoji is to textspeak what kinesics and paralanguage are to spoken language." Evans disagrees with those who believe that emojis represent "a step backwards to the dark ages of illiteracy, making us poorer communicators" (p. 136). Emojis seem especially useful for quickly connecting and coordinating with others, rather than for serious and longform writing. In the right situations, using an emoji "actually enables users to better express their emotions... [and] become more effective digital communicators" (Evans 2017:137).

Evans' work does not directly draw on the sociology of emotions. However, we can extrapolate from his book and perhaps deepen his analysis. Evans' argument seems to be that people use emojis to depict their emotions strategically, in order to have a desired effect on their audiences. That's *impression management*, a central topic of this book. Recall that *surface acting* (Chapter 3) overlaps partially with *emotional identification* (Chapter 6). People can label their feelings ("I love the sweater you gave me, grandma!") in order to shape the way that others think and feel about them, a behavior that is simultaneously emotion management and emotional identification. Now let's apply those ideas to Evans' work. It seems likely that people often use *emojis* to hide, disguise, or at least selectively reveal their feelings, just as they do with statements like "I *love* the sweater." For example, someone may end a note with a smiley face to give the impression of positivity or happiness when in reality they feel ambivalent or disappointed. Or, we might text "I'm excited to come to your party" and reinforce that statement with emojis (thumbs up, party hat, champagne bottle), even though seconds earlier we were considering whether we could come up with a plausible excuse to decline the invitation.

Let's make a few more connections to emotional identification that Evans' book brings to mind. From earlier in this chapter, recall how different cultures *create and promote* different vocabularies of emotion: I might be inclined to use one of only eight emotion words if raised among the Chewong; to embrace the metaphor "I could blow a gale" if I was angry and spoke Zulu; to invoke the label "hysterical" if I were socialized into the customs of a 9-1-1 call center. Plus, earlier we discussed how our companions can *coach* us towards certain labels, such as when they ask "Are you nervous or excited...?" By building on those ideas, I think we could argue that software developers create, promote, and coach us into using standardized emoji options. Platforms may nudge people towards using software-preferred emotional depictions rather than simply enabling users to "better express their emotions" (as Evans put). For example, when texting on my smart phone, I can click on a button that displays my most frequently used emojis. There I can quickly find the smiley and angry face emojis. That ease of access means I am more likely to portray my feelings via those signs rather than searching through the 100+ face options I currently have—even though one of those options might be more specific and accurate. Also, we should note that those 100+ options are far fewer than the 2,000+ emotion terms that English speakers potentially have at their disposal. Thus, I think we could ask questions like: If it weren't for the all-too-accessible smiley and angry face emojis, wouldn't some people otherwise be inclined to describe themselves via written categories such as content, pleased, or elated (on the one hand) vs. mad, upset, or frustrated (on the other)? And some of these categories could create much different meanings and interactional consequences than the quickly selected smiley or angry face. Thus, my point is that the opportunities and constraints provided in digital environments are yet another social factor that shapes the way emotional identification proceeds. Some scholars use the concept *affordances* to describe this phenomenon: social media technology offers resources and limitations for enacting emotions in particular ways (Bareither 2019).

Identifying emotion is an understudied phenomenon in sociology, particularly when compared to the huge literature on emotional labor. Far fewer scholars have set out to examine the practice of labeling what we and others feel. That trend has held true for emerging digital environments, even though emotional identification is very common online. Perhaps you'll want to help remedy that neglect, starting with a course assignment or exercise? See the prompt at the end of this chapter.

7) Emotional Identification and Emotional Labor

As we've already seen in this chapter, emotional identification overlaps with surface acting and deep acting. Nervous public speakers who claim they are "very happy to be here" may be managing how they appear to feel by strategically labeling their emotions. On the other hand, hikers who see a bear in the woods may attempt to actually suppress fear by telling themselves "How exciting!" (rather than "How scary!"), using strategic labeling as a form of cognitive deep acting (see Hochschild 1983:206; Thoits 1985:235).

Emotional identification also overlaps with emotional labor (defined as paid emotion management) in many respects (Harris 2010). As a part of their daily routines, employees may attempt to identify what customers are feeling, in order to take appropriate steps to keep them satisfied. For example, a waiter may exclaim "That table is getting frustrated with me!" in order to motivate herself or to encourage the cooks to hurry up. Employers, too, may adopt or encourage the use of particular categories of emotion, in order to attract customers and spur employee performance. Consider this advertisement, which I downloaded from the "career opportunities" link on the website of a prominent hotel:

> At Outrigger Hotels and Resorts we look for people who embrace the cultures and communities where they live, who actively learn from others, and who, in turn, warmly share their knowledge and experiences with co-workers and guests. We admire individuals who strive to always do their

best, who are motivated by teamwork, and who treat others with fairness and respect. ... Most importantly, we are a company that practices *aloha*. Every one of our [*staff*] needs to feel *aloha* and genuinely extend *aloha* to all, be they guests or colleagues, strangers or friends.[8]

Here, the concept of "aloha" is portrayed as a type of emotion that must be felt by any prospective employee, no matter what city, state, or country they are from. This feeling cannot merely be displayed through surface acting but must be "genuinely" extended to everyone a worker meets. Presumably, the feeling of aloha is one of warmth and affection—an attitude that welcomes people into one's life rather than seeing them as "other" or as an annoying burden. The hotel is seeking to create a company culture that sponsors (if not dictates) particular emotion norms *and* categories.

Many workplaces encourage institutionally preferred emotional vocabularies. Salespeople may be encouraged to express and show the "pride" they feel in their company and its products (Ash 1984, ch. 14). Financial advisors[9] may be encouraged to tell clients that "No one, without your last name, will care more about your financial success than I will." A 9-1-1 call taker might be taught to use the label "hysterical" in written reports of callers' behavior, as opposed to "scared," "worried," or "in shock" (Whalen and Zimmerman 1998). A family therapist may use a pre-printed poster or handout providing a list of emotion states for clients to choose from (Gubrium 1992). In all these situations, emotional labeling may be being guided by the local culture of the workplace. Once again, individuals' descriptions of their emotional states may be the result of social processes, rather than spontaneous or straightforward statements of fact.

Exercises

1 Analyze an instance of emotional identification. (A) First, observe a social interaction in your everyday life or on television. Write down exactly what was said, as best as you can. Also take notes on the context—such as who was present, and when and where the behavior occurred. (B) Connect your example to at least two of the social dimensions of emotional identification that were discussed in this chapter. It's OK to discuss what did happen as well as what could have happened (hypothetically), in order to make your points.
2 Review this chapter's Spotlight on Research. Based on that discussion, can you describe and analyze one or more examples of emoji use by yourself or someone you know? Try to focus on instances where emojis are used to depict or describe feelings. Do you think surface acting may be occurring? Would the person characterize their own feelings differently if they were describing feelings in person rather than online? Also, Evans (2017) argues that emojis assist in clear communication. But can you identify a time when you used an emoji that was misinterpreted by a family member, classmate, or friend?

Notes

1. In section #6 of this chapter, we'll return to the topic of "who knows best" about emotions and will ask whether the experiencing individual is necessarily the best authority on his or her feelings.
2. Not all sensations are emotional, either (Averill 1974:176). For example, we might tremble due to due to hyperthermia rather than fear.
3. The phrase "out of" can be given different meanings depending on the context. Sometimes people say they act "out of love," meaning their behavior is motivated by the presence of that emotion, not its absence.
4. Java is an island in Indonesia.
5. See Best and Furedi (2001) on road rage, Berns (2011) on closure, and we can thank actors Mike Myers and Dana Carvey for schwing (see the 1992 movie *Wayne's World*). Schwing is a metaphor that compares the penis to a sword; the word approximates the sound of a blade being withdrawn from its metal scabbard (or sheath). Whether that is a happy metaphor, I leave to readers to decide. The gag certainly prompted laughter and amusement in the early 1990s.
6. Chagga is a Bantu language spoken on Mount Kilimanjaro in Tanzania.
7. A catchy 1980s song by Duran Duran once characterized lust as being "Hungry like the Wolf." Check it out on YouTube.com. Since then, Nicky Minaj and Sir Mix-a-Lot both have recorded songs about male lust as the desire of an "anaconda" (metaphorical penis) to bite into large female buttocks.
8. Downloaded August 11, 2023, from www.outrigger.com/about-us/career-opportunities. Italics added.
9. This promise used to appear verbatim on the websites of multiple financial advisors who worked for Wells Fargo, such as www.chucknovy.com/The-Five-Ground-Rules.8.htm and www.pdearcangelis.wfadv.com/Our-Five-Ground-Rules.4.htm (downloaded October 28, 2014). A modified version of this statement, "No one without your last name will care more about you and your future than we do," can be found at www.raymondjames.com/meinrodleeper/about-us (downloaded August 10, 2023).

Suggested Readings

Nancy Berns's delightful book takes an insightful, humorous, and poignant look at the creation and proliferation of "closure" as an emotion category. The first chapter provides a history of closure's ascendance in the US, while subsequent chapters explore its use by doctors, lawyers, politicians, psychics, salespeople, divorcees, and the bereaved, among others.

Berns, Nancy. 2011. *Closure: The Rush to End Grief and What It Costs Us*. Philadelphia, PA: Temple.

Michele Emanatian provides a succinct and intriguing example of research on emotion metaphors. She focuses on the ways "lust" is characterized in two different languages. Zoltan Kövecses, a leading scholar in the study of emotion metaphors, provides a more wide-ranging analysis.

Emanatian, Michele. 1995. "Metaphor and the Expression of Emotion: The Value of Cross-Cultural Perspectives." *Metaphor and Symbolic Activity* 10:163–182. https://doi.org/10.1207/s15327868ms1003_2

Kövecses, Zoltán. 2000. *Metaphor and Emotion: Language, Culture, and Body in Human Feeling*. New York: Cambridge University Press.

Readers who enjoyed Chapter 3's discussion of Shane Sharp's (2010) research may appreciate Amy Wilkins' work. Wilkins studied an international organization that recruits students on college campuses. Members of this organization are taught that perceiving and describing oneself as "happy" is essential to being a true Christian.

Wilkins, Amy C. 2008. "'Happier than Non-Christians': Collective Emotions and Symbolic Boundaries among Evangelical Christians." *Social Psychology Quarterly* 71:281–301. https://doi.org/10.1177/019027250807100308

Kerry Ferris and I conducted an accessible study of emotional identification by celebrities and entertainment journalists in *Stargazing: Celebrity, Fame, and Social Interaction*. Emotions are a frequent topic in the red-carpet interviews that take place just prior to award shows. Entertainment journalists ask how stars are feeling as they enter the auditorium: Are you happy to be here? Excited? Nervous? Ferris and I collected 317 of these televised interactions and analyzed them using concepts described earlier in this chapter.

Ferris, Kerry O. and Scott R. Harris. 2011. *Stargazing: Celebrity, Fame, and Social Interaction*. New York: Routledge. (See the fifth chapter especially.)

Readers who want to follow up on this chapter's Spotlight on Research could take a look at Wang and Haapio-Kirk's qualitative study of emojis and other digital images in computer-mediated interaction. The authors analyze examples of emotional identification and surface acting on two social media platforms: WeChat in China and LINE in Japan.

Wang, Xinyuan and Laura Haapio-Kirk. 2021. "Emotion Work via Digital Visual Communication: A Comparative Study between China and Japan." *Global Media and China* 6(3):325–344. https://doi.org/10.1177/20594364211008044

7 Why Study the Sociology of Emotions?

The preceding chapters of this book have provided a basic—and very selective—glimpse into the sociology of emotions. For someone who is new to this area of research, it might seem as though we have covered a lot of ground. Actually, we have only scratched the surface. I have neglected many classic and contemporary studies of the book's central topics—emotion norms, management, exchanges, labor, and identification. Moreover, I have ignored other sociological perspectives that animate the field, such as affect control theory, expectation states theory, identity theory, and ritual theories (see Stets and Turner 2014). I also left out work by sociologists who draw heavily from outside the discipline, such as psychoanalysis (Scheff 2016) as well as evolutionary theory and neuroscience (Franks 2014; Turner 2022). There are scholars who focus on emotions in general whereas others give extended treatment to a single emotion such as pride, shame, anxiety, fear, loneliness, and so on (see the edited collection by Jacobsen (2023b). Thus, readers who enjoy this textbook could seek out a deeper and broader exposure to the field.[1] A select few readers might even want to write an undergraduate thesis on the topic or specialize in the study of emotions in graduate school. Others may be content simply to "live with" (and "test out" in their daily lives) the concepts they've acquired from this book.

The sociology of emotions is a diverse field that can offer different things to different people. In the final few pages that remain, I will outline seven reasons why readers might enjoy or benefit from studying the social dimensions of emotions—through this book and beyond it.

1. Emotions Are Always a Relevant—and Potentially Fun—Topic

One reason to learn about the sociology of emotions is because it's a topic that is *always pertinent to one's life*. No offense intended to professors who teach calculus, French, international politics, or ancient history, but not all subjects can claim such immediate and observable relevance to our everyday lives. Even casual observation lends support to the notion that emotions pervade and color most if not all our social interactions. In virtually any setting, it is

DOI: 10.4324/b23334-7

relatively easy to see people managing emotions in order to conform to norms or to negotiate their social exchanges. Emotional identification is commonplace as well. Co-workers and friends routinely portray themselves as happy, frustrated, worried, thrilled, or sorry, through surface acting and through emotional identification. Turn on the news and you'll likely see politicians labeling their own feelings ("I love this country") and others' feelings ("Americans are nervous about inflation"). Whenever I teach about emotions, I can always incorporate a fresh batch of compelling incidents to examine.

Arguably, it's easier to maintain interest in a topic when fascinating examples arise so frequently. What could be more fun than to develop a deeper appreciation for, and intelligence about, the feelings that make our daily lives so joyful and so miserable?

2. Seeing the Familiar in a New Light

Emotions may be ubiquitous, but their familiarity can (ironically) lead us to overlook them—like fish who take water for granted. Before finishing Chapter 6, readers may not have given much thought to statements such as "I'm happy to be here" or "I love pizza." The smile flashed by a McDonald's cashier may have meant little to you, until after you have read Chapter 5 on emotional labor. You may have felt irritated by a friend's poor display of sympathy but did not have the conceptual tools of exchange theory to explain your dissatisfaction over the lack of reciprocity. Thus, for me and many of my students, the main appeal of sociological concepts is that they enable you to see and analyze behaviors that previously had escaped your notice, even instances that were right before your eyes (Berger 1963).

Proponents of public health remind us that certain activities—such as exercising and eating vegetables—can "add years to your life." Somewhat similarly, I like to say that reading sociology can "add life to your years," by giving you so many intriguing things to think about. No interaction is boring if you bring the right set of concepts to the occasion.

3. Drawing Connections between Disparate Realms

Sociological concepts make familiar activities seem novel and interesting. They also help us draw parallels between situations that seem diverse and unrelated. By focusing on generic social processes, we can learn about recurring behaviors that cut across time and place (Grills 2020; Prus 1996).

Surface acting, deep acting, emotional labor, and similar notions can be used to draw parallels between persons and places that seem quite disconnected, such as professors, salespeople, athletes, detectives, exotic dancers, and doctors. All these people may engage in similar forms of behavior, even though the specific content of their behavior may differ. For example, both doctors and exotic dancers may use cognitive deep acting to redefine what nudity means, in order to carry out their work unencumbered by embarrassment. Or, professors, salespersons, and athletes may generate enthusiasm (or quiet nerves) by using bodily deep acting, before they enter a classroom, make a sales pitch, or take the field.

A sociological mindset relishes cultural diversity as well as recurring patterns. The right concept, such as interactional coaching (from Chapter 6), can help a person notice parallels between interactions and settings that are quite distinct in many ways.

4. Learning about the World, and Yourself, Simultaneously

I have found that some of my students are slightly narcissistic or self-absorbed. They want to know: What do these ideas have to do with me? Can they help me understand myself better? Will I be able to navigate my relationships more successfully? Other students are more outward-looking. They want to know: What's going on in the world? Why do people do what they do? How does this research help me understand the thoughts, feelings, and actions of particular types of people or of human beings in general?

Whether you tend to be inward-looking, outward-looking, or both, the sociology of emotions can fit your interests. For example, as I read Hochschild's (1983) research on bill collectors, I learn more about that profession and gain insight into my own career, simultaneously. Bill collectors must create alarm in order to motivate people to pay overdue bills, while responding to potentially genuine reasons for delays (e.g., I became sick and couldn't work). If I want to, I can focus on the specific details of this occupation and learn about the nuanced emotional labor that bill collectors must perform. On the other hand, I can turn inward, and draw connections to myself. As a professor, I too must manage the emotions as I create alarm about term-paper due-dates or respond to student's stories of ill health and bad luck. I can explore overlaps in the surface and deep-acting strategies that bill collectors and professors use, even as I tease out differences.

Sociologists of emotions conduct research on a wide range of dilemmas that may impact you personally or shape the lives of others you care about. These dilemmas may be relatively minor—such as coping with interactional discord (Albas and Albas 1988a; Harris 1997)—or incredibly significant—such as dealing with domestic violence, homicide, or rape (Goodrum 2008; Kolb 2011; Konradi 1999). Either way, it can be educating, comforting, and empowering to learn about those dilemmas from sociologists of emotion. Such researchers provide accessible, interesting, and data-based insights without oversimplifying, preaching, or individualizing problems as some "self-help" guides tend to do.

5. Developing Valuable Skills

In some courses, sociology students acquire technical skills. For example, coursework on research methods teaches students to collect and analyze data in a systematic fashion. Most of the time, though, sociology fosters skills that are "softer" (yet still very important), such as the ability to think critically and deeply about how social forces shape our lives. Studying the sociology of emotions promotes these same skills, and more.

There are many definitions of critical thinking—which is not simply "being mean." To think critically involves practices such as uncovering hidden assumptions; questioning received wisdoms and customs; and evaluating arguments based on logic and evidence. These are all skills that can grow out of a serious engagement with sociological research on emotions.

For example, in everyday life people tend to assume the "naturalness" of emotion norms when they make claims about people's behavior. Individuals may argue that we (or someone we know) are acting strangely, if not immorally or unprofessionally. Such arguments may or may not have validity, but before formulating a serious response, a critical thinker may want to examine the cultural assumptions undergirding them.

As we saw in Chapter 2, emotion norms may seem simply "logical," but they are created by groups, and thus vary by time and place. A behavior may be interpreted as "inappropriate" for subjective cultural reasons as much or more than for objective considerations of its consequences. Moreover, as we saw in Chapter 5, emotion norms may be inequitably applied to women and people of color, which is a further factor that a critical thinker may want to consider. Similarly, Chapter 6 showed how any emotional description is a claim, one that can be upgraded, downgraded, or rejected entirely, for a variety of reasons.

The sociology of emotions thus reinforces relatively standard sociological skill sets, including (but not limited to) critical thinking. Arguably, research in this area goes further by giving students the opportunity to develop their intra- and interpersonal emotion management skills.

Reading this book and its suggested readings may leave a person better equipped to (a) identify the relevant emotion norms that people use to evaluate their conduct; (b) envision a range of surface and deep-acting strategies that can be used to conform to the norms; and (c) articulate an argument for changing the norms. Per Chapters 3 and 6, these skills certainly can be used for dishonest and strictly self-serving purposes. On the other hand—and what will hopefully be the case—the skills can be used for good.

For example, suppose you want to clearly convey your disappointment or love to a family member. Thinking more precisely about potential surface-acting strategies (e.g., words, tone of voice, facial expressions, clothing) and deep-acting strategies (cognitive, bodily, and expressive) can help you be more creative, thorough, and effective as you navigate that personal relationship. Similarly, a stressful situation at work might be more effectively analyzed and handled by a person who can draw on the conceptual apparatus of the sociology of emotions, as my sixth point explains below.

6. Preparing for and Advancing in One's Career

Entering "sociology of emotions" into the search engine of a job website (such as Indeed.com or Monster.com) will yield few helpful results. Looking for similar key words in "help wanted" sections of a local newspaper will generate even fewer leads. At first glance, it seems no one is hiring individuals with expertise in this topic.

On the other hand, there are at least two reasons why learning about the sociology of emotions could be advantageous on the job market. It can help you become more familiar with (a) the careers that are available and (b) what it takes to succeed within those occupations.

Many people (especially college students) do not know exactly what they want to do with their lives. Reading the literature on emotional labor can provide a fascinating glimpse into the daily concerns and activities that accompany particular careers. When I first read Stenross and Kleinman's (1989) research on detectives, for example, I was struck by the tediousness of the report writing, which is so seldom shown in television dramas (see also Phillips 2016).Though I had anticipated the difficulty of comforting victims of crime, I did not expect to learn that victims can create additional emotional-labor demands, by telling detectives how to do their jobs, by providing incomplete or inaccurate information, by failing to show up at court, and by neglecting to express gratitude. All these actions tend to make a detective's job more difficult, increasing the need to suppress frustration or to motivate victims to help more.

By recounting this example I am not encouraging readers to overgeneralize; a single study cannot capture all the dimensions of an occupation, and experiences vary for different workers. However, reading a case study of emotional labor is certainly far better than obtaining career guidance from (for example) simply watching television. Additional readings can supplement one's understanding of a career and allow for comparisons across different paths that a student is considering. A person who wants to investigate or excel at a particular occupation would be wise to read the literature that sociologists of emotion have produced on that occupation (and on similar jobs). Such studies—which are often based on interviews with dozens of practitioners—usually attempt to uncover the emotion management strategies that workers use to overcome the recurring dilemmas that they face. Such information seems highly informative and practical.

Let's also recall Exercise #2, from Chapter 5. There I encouraged readers to conduct informational interviews as a way to learn about a career option. As part of a class assignment—or on one's own initiative—interviewing people about their emotional labor can provide revealing insights into the daily work routines (and demands) of some jobs compared to others. Because emotional labor is often taken for granted, workers may not be prepared to deal with the emotional demands of their occupations, as Martin (2005:212) found with rape workers: "Physicians, nurses, prosecutors, police officers, judges, defense attorneys, and even victim advocates trained in the instrumental tasks of their professions are rarely prepared for the emotions of a traumatized individual who has been violated in the most intimate way. They do not know how to handle a rape victim nor their reactions to her and her experience." To an equivalent or lesser degree, the same might be said of the emotional demands made in many other occupations. Thus, a great amount of foresight and understanding might be gained by reading what sociologists of emotion have written about the career paths you consider pursuing.

7. Understanding Inequality

Many students are drawn to sociology for its attention to social justice. Throughout the history of the discipline, many if not most scholars have exhibited a concern with understanding and/or ameliorating the negative effects of social inequality. Courses on social stratification are clearly about inequality, but so too are those that focus on other topics. Any subject of sociological research—crime, education, family, immigration—tends to deal with inequalities of gender, race, and class, among other forms of disparity. Interestingly, membership in the sociology honor society Alpha Kappa Delta requires a commitment to serving others.[2]

As we saw in Chapters 2 and 5, the topic of emotions connects quite clearly with social inequality. Women, workers of color, and all those with lower "status shields" are often required to perform more emotional labor than others do. Emotional laborers must conform to emotion norms set by employers and adapt to company instructions for surface and deep-acting strategies ("Remember to always smile!" "The customer is always right!"). Unpaid labor, in the form of kin work, is also unequally distributed, as women provide more nurturing and care to members of their immediate and extended families.

Additional readings in the sociology of emotions highlight further examples of intersections between emotions and inequality. For example, Schwalbe et al. (2000) argued that elites often manipulate emotions in order to keep subordinates from challenging the status quo. Individuals who are encouraged to attribute success to hard work and talent are less likely to experience or express anger towards those who inherit vast advantages through wealth and family connections. Instead of focusing on such disparities, workers may simply "try harder" and blame only themselves for any lack of success. Shame and other negative feelings are frequently neglected outcomes of social class. A careful consideration of emotions can thus illuminate the subjective experience of inequality, beyond the "cold hard facts" that charts and statistics reveal (see also Clark 1997, ch. 7; Collins 2000).

Conclusion

In this chapter I have outlined seven potential benefits of studying the sociology of emotions. I encourage readers to treat my list as a conversation starter, rather than the final word. After reading this book, it should be relatively easy for you to imagine arguments and examples that may bolster—or challenge—these points.

Not everybody will, or must, enjoy the sociology of emotions. But for those who see the appeal, studying the social dimensions of emotions can be a profoundly compelling, relevant, useful, and moral endeavor.

Notes

1 In Chapter 1, I also mentioned that emotions have been studied by scholars from other disciplines as well, such as those working in anthropology, communication, geography, history, and psychology. Recommended readings appear at the end of that chapter.
2 See http://alphakappadelta.org.

Bibliography

Al-Shawaf, Laith and David M. G. Lewis. 2017. "Evolutionary Psychology and the Emotions." Pp. 1–9 in *Encyclopedia of Personality and Individual Differences*, edited by Virgil Zeigler-Hill and Todd K. Shackelford. Cham, Switzerland: Springer.

Albas, Daniel and Cheryl. Albas. 1988a. "Aces and Bombers: The Post-Exam Impression Management Strategies of Students." *Symbolic Interaction* 11(2):289–302. https://doi.org/10.1525/si.1988.11.2.289

Albas, Cheryl and Daniel Albas. 1988b. "Emotion Work and Emotion Rules: The Case of Exams." *Qualitative Sociology* 11:259–274. https://doi.org/10.1007/BF00988966

Adler, Patricia A. and Peter Adler. 2011. *The Tender Cut: Inside the Hidden World of Self-Injury*. New York: NYU Press.

Arcy, Jacquelyn. 2016. "Emotion Work: Considering Gender in Digital Labor." *Feminist Media Studies* 16(2):365–368. DOI: 10.1080/14680777.2016.1138609

Arluke, Arnold. 1998. "Managing Emotions in an Animal Shelter." Pp. 254–266 in *Inside Social Life* (2nd Ed.), edited by Spencer Cahill. Los Angeles: Roxbury.

Ash, Mary K. 1984. *Mary Kay on People Management*. New York: Warner Books.

Ashkanasy, Neal M. and Catherine S. Daus. 2002. "Emotion in the Workplace: The New Challenge for Managers." *Academy of Management Executive* 16(1):76–86.

Averill, James R. 1974. "An Analysis of Psychophysiological Symbolism and Its Influence on Theories of Emotion." *Journal for the Theory of Social Behaviour* 4(2):147–190. https://doi.org/10.1111/j.1468-5914.1974.tb00336.x

Bachen, Christine M. and Eva Illouz. 1996. "Imagining Romance: Young People's Cultural Models of Romance and Love." *Critical Studies in Mass Communication* 13(4):279–308. https://doi.org/10.1080/15295039609366983

Bareither, Christoph. 2019. "Doing Emotion through Digital Media: An Ethnographic Perspective on Media Practices and Emotional Affordances." *Ethnologia Europaea* 49(1):7–23. https://doi.org/10.16995/ee.822

Barrett, Lisa Feldman. 2006. "Solving the Emotion Paradox: Categorization and the Experience of Emotion." *Personality and Social Psychology Review* 10:20–46. https://doi.org/10.1207/s15327957pspr1001_2

Bellas, Marcia L. 1999. "Emotional Labor in Academia: The Case of Professors." *Annals of the American Academy of Political and Social Science* 561:96–110. https://doi.org/10.1177/000271629956100107

Bellas, Marcia L. 2001. "The Gendered Nature of Emotional Labor in the Workplace." Pp. 269–278 in *Gender Mosaics*, edited by Dana Vannoy. Los Angeles: Roxbury.

Bergman Blix, Stina and Åsa Wettergren. 2018. *Professional Emotions in Court: A Sociological Perspective*. New York: Routledge.

Berns, Nancy. 2011. *Closure: The Rush to End Grief and What It Costs Us*. Philadelphia, PA: Temple University Press.

Berger, Peter. 1963. *Invitation to Sociology*. Garden City, NY: Anchor Books.

Best, Joel. and Frank Furedi. 2001. "The Evolution of Road Rage in Britain and the United States." Pp. 107–127 in *How Claims Spread: Cross-National Diffusion of Social Problems*, edited by Joel Best. New York: Aldine de Gruyter.

Blau, Peter M. 1964. *Exchange and Power in Social Life*. New York: Wiley.

Bloch, Charlotte. 2012. *Passion and Paranoia: Emotions and the Culture of Emotion in Academia*. Burlington, VT: Ashgate.

Blumer, Herbert. 1969. *Symbolic Interactionism: Perspective and Method*. Englewood Cliffs, NJ: Prentice-Hall.

Briggs, Jean L. 1970. *Never in Anger: Portrait of an Eskimo Family*. Cambridge, MA: Harvard University Press.

Brownlie, Julie and Frances Shaw. 2019. "Empathy Rituals: Small Conversations about Emotional Distress on Twitter." *Sociology* 53(1):104–122. https://doi.org/10.1177/0038038518767075

Cahill, Spencer E. 1999. "Emotional Capital and Professional Socialization: The Case of Mortuary Science Students (and Me)." *Social Psychology Quarterly* 62(2):101–116. https://doi.org/10.2307/2695852

Cahill, Spencer E. and Robin Eggleston. 1994. "Managing Emotions in Public: The Case of Wheelchair Users." *Social Psychology Quarterly* 57:300–312. https://doi.org/10.2307/2787157

Cain, Susan. 2012. *Quiet: The Power of Introverts in a World that Can't Stop Talking*. New York: Crown.

Casioppo, Danielle. 2020. "The Cultivation of Joy: Practices from the Buddhist Tradition, Positive Psychology, and Yogic Philosophy." *The Journal of Positive Psychology* 15(1):67–73. https://doi.org/10.1080/17439760.2019.1685577

Chandler, Amy. 2012. "Self-Injury as Embodied Emotion Work: Managing Rationality, Emotions and Bodies." *Sociology* 46(3):442–457. https://doi.org/10.1177/0038038511422589

Chavez, Sergio, Robin Paige, and Heather Edelblute. 2023. "Emotion Work and Gender Inequality in Transnational Family Life." *Journal of Family Issues* 44(3):703–724. https://doi.org/10.1177/0192513X211054472

Clanton, Gordon. 1989. "Jealousy in American Culture, 1945–1985: Reflections from Popular Literature." Pp. 179–193 in *The Sociology of Emotions: Original Essays and Research Papers*, edited by David D. Franks and E. Doyle McCarthy. Greenwich, CT: JAI.

Clanton, Gordon. 2006. "Jealousy and Envy." Pp. 410–442 in *Handbook of the Sociology of Emotions*, edited by Jonthan H. Turner and Jan E. Stets. New York: Springer.

Clark, Candace. 1987. "Sympathy Biography and Sympathy Margin." *American Journal of Sociology* 93(2):290–321. https://doi.org/10.1086/228746

Clark, Candace. 1997. *Misery and Company: Sympathy in Everyday Life*. Chicago: University of Chicago Press.

Clark, Candace. 2002. "Taming the 'Brute Being': Sociology Reckons with Emotionality." Pp. 155–182 in *Postmodern Existential Sociology*, edited by Joseph A. Kotarba and John M. Johnson. Walnut Creek, CA: AltaMira.

Clark, Candace. 2004. "Emotional Gifts and 'You First' Micropolitics: Niceness in the Socioemotional Economy." Pp. 402–421 in *Feelings and Emotions: The Amsterdam Symposium*, edited by Antony S. R. Manstead, Nico Frijda, and Agneta Fischer. New York: Cambridge University Press.

Cottingham, Marci D., Austin H. Johnson, and Rebecca J. Erickson. 2018. "'I Can Never Be Too Comfortable': Race, Gender, and Emotion at the Hospital Bedside." *Qualitative Health Research* 28(1):145–158.

Collins, Randall. 2000. "Situational Stratification: A Micro-Macro Theory of Inequality." *Sociological Theory* 18:17–43. https://doi.org/10.1111/0735-2751.00086

Copp, Martha. 1998. "When Emotion Work Is Doomed to Fail: Ideological and Structural Constraints on Emotion Management." *Symbolic Interaction* 21:299–328. https://doi.org/10.1525/si.1998.21.3.299

Coupland, Christine, Andrew D. Brown, Kevin Daniels, and Michael Humphreys. 2008. "Saying It with Feeling: Analysing Speakable Emotions." *Human Relations* 61(3):327–353. https://doi.org/10.1177/0018726708088997

Crabtree, Arialle K. and Patricia Richards. 2021. "Feeling Rules in the Marriage Equality Movement: Public Protest, Social Media and the Management of Emotion." *Queer Studies in Media & Popular Culture* 6(1):73–90. https://doi.org/10.1386/qsmpc_00045_1

Danesi, Marcel. 2017. *The Semiotics of Emoji: The Rise of Visual Language in the Age of the Internet*. New York: Bloomsbury Publishing. Kindle Edition.

Davis, Joseph E. 2012. "Emotions as Commentaries on Cultural Norms." Ch. 2 in *The Emotions and Cultural Analysis*, edited by Ana Marta González. Burlington, VT: Ashgate.

Delaney, Kevin J. 2012. *Money at Work: On the Job with Priests, Poker Players, and Hedge Fund Traders*. New York: NYU Press.

Derks, Daantje, Agneta H. Fischer, and Arjan E. R. Bos. 2008. "The Role of Emotion in Computer-Mediated Communication: A Review." *Computers in Human Behavior* 24(3):766–785. https://doi.org/10.1016/j.chb.2007.04.004

Derné, Steve. 1994. "Structural Realities, Persistent Dilemmas, and the Construction of Emotional Paradigms: Love in Three Cultures." Pp. 281–308 in *Social Perspectives on Emotion* (Vol. II), edited by William M. Wentworth and John Ryan. Greenwich, CT: JAI.

Deshotels, Tina and Craig J. Forsyth. 2006. "Strategic Flirting and the Emotional Tab of Exotic Dancing." *Deviant Behavior* 27(2):223–241. https://doi.org/10.1080/01639620500468600

Deutsch, Francine M. 1999. *Halving It All: How Equally Shared Parenting Works*. Cambridge, MA: Harvard.

Devault, Marjorie L. 1991. *Feeding the Family*. Chicago: University of Chicago Press.

Dixon, Thomas. 2012. "'Emotion': The History of a Keyword in Crisis." *Emotion Review* 4(4):338–344. https://doi.org/10.1177/1754073912445814

Edwards, Derek. 1999. "Emotion Discourse." *Culture & Psychology* 5(3):271–291. https://doi.org/10.1177/1354067X9953001

Ellis, Carolyn. 1991. "Sociological Introspection and Emotional Experience." *Symbolic Interaction* 14(1):23–50. https://doi.org/10.1525/si.1991.14.1.23

Ellis, Colter and Leslie Irvine. 2010. "Reproducing Dominion: Emotional Apprenticeship in the 4-H Youth Livestock Program." *Society and Animals* 18:21–39. DOI: 10.1163/106311110X12586086158402

Emanatian, Michele. 1995. "Metaphor and the Expression of Emotion: The Value of Cross-Cultural Perspectives." *Metaphor and Symbolic Activity* 10:163–182. https://doi.org/10.1207/s15327868ms1003_2

Emerson, Joan P. 2001. "Behavior in Private Places: Sustaining Definitions of Reality in Gynecological Examinations." Pp. 265–278 in *The Production of Reality* (3rd Ed.), edited by Jodi O'Brien and Peter Kollock. Thousand Oaks, CA: Pine Forge Press.

Enarson, Elaine. 1993. "Emotion Workers on the Production Line: The Feminizing of Casino Card Dealing." *NWSA Journal* 5:218–232.

Erickson, Rebecca J. and Marci D. Cottingham. 2014. "Emotions and Families." Pp. 359–383 in *Handbook of the Sociology of Emotions* (Vol. II), edited by Jan E. Stets and Jonthan H. Turner. New York: Springer.

Erickson, Rebecca J. and Wendy J. C. Grove. 2008. "Emotional Labor and Health Care." *Sociology Compass* 2:704–733. https://doi.org/10.1111/j.1751-9020.2007.00084.x

Esala, Jennifer J. and Jared Del Rosso. 2020. "Emotions into Disorder: Anxiety Disorders and the Social Meaning of Fear." *Symbolic Interaction* 43(2):235–256. https://doi.org/10.1002/symb.450

Evans, Louwanda. 2013. *Cabin Pressure: African American Pilots, Flight Attendants, and Emotional Labor.* Lanham, MD: Rowman and Littlefield.

Evans, Louwanda and Wendy L. Moore. 2015. "Impossible Burdens: White Institutions, Emotional Labor, and Micro-Resistance." *Social Problems* 62:439–454. https://doi.org/10.1093/socpro/spv009

Evans, Vyvyan. 2017. *The Emoji Code: The Linguistics Behind Smiley Faces and Scaredy Cats.* New York: Picador. Kindle Edition.

Feagin, Joe R. 2010. *Racist America: Roots, Current Realities, and Future Reparations* (2nd Ed.). New York: Routledge.

Ferris, Kerry O. and Scott R. Harris. 2011. *Stargazing: Celebrity, Fame, and Social Interaction.* New York: Routledge.

Fine, Gary Alan, Beth Montemurro, Bonnie Semora, Marybeth C. Stalp, Dane S. Claussen, and Zayda Sierra. 1998. "Social Order through a Prism: Color as Collective Representation." *Sociological Inquiry* 68(4):443–457. https://doi.org/10.1111/j.1475-682X.1998.tb00479.x

Flower, Lisa. 2018. "Doing Loyalty: Defense Lawyers' Subtle Dramas in the Courtroom." *Journal of Contemporary Ethnography* 47(2):226–254. https://doi.org/10.1177/0891241616646826

Francis, Linda E. 1994. "Laughter, the Best Mediation: Humor as Emotion Management in Interaction." *Symbolic Interaction* 17(2):147–163. https://doi.org/10.1525/si.1994.17.2.147

Franks, David. 1994. "The Etymology of Emotion." Pp. 38–41 in *Sociology of Emotions: Syllabi and Instructional Material*, edited by Catherine G. Valentine and Steve Derné. Washington, DC: American Sociological Association.

Franks, David. 2014. "Emotions and Neurosociology." Pp. 267–281 in *Handbook of the Sociology of Emotions* (Vol. II), edited by Jan E. Stets and Jonathan H. Turner. New York: Springer.

Gallmeier, Charles P. 1987. "Putting on the Game Face: The Staging of Emotions in Professional Hockey." *Sociology of Sport Journal* 4:347–362. DOI: https://doi.org/10.1123/ssj.4.4.347

Goddard, Cliff. 2002. "Explicating Emotions across Languages and Cultures: A Semantic Approach." Pp. 19–53 in *The Verbal Communication of Emotion: Interdisciplinary Perspectives*, edited by Susan R. Fussell. Mahwah, NJ: Lawrence Erlbaum.

Goffman, Erving. 1952. "On Cooling the Mark Out: Some Aspects of Adaptation to Failure." *Psychiatry* 15(4):451–463. https://doi.org/10.1080/00332747.1952.11022896

Goffman, Erving. 1959. *The Presentation of Self in Everyday Life*. New York: Doubleday.

Goffman, Erving. 1963. *Behavior in Public Places*. New York: Free Press.

Goodrum, Sarah. 2008. "When the Management of Grief Becomes Everyday Life: The Aftermath of Murder." *Symbolic Interaction* 31(4):422–442. https://doi.org/10.1525/si.2008.31.4.422

Goodrum, Sarah and Mark C. Stafford. 2003. "The Management of Emotions in the Criminal Justice System." *Sociological Focus* 36:179–196. https://doi.org/10.1080/00380237.2003.10570723

Gordon, Steven L. 1989. "The Socialization of Children's Emotions: Emotional Culture, Competence, and Exposure." Pp. 319–349 in *Children's Understanding of Emotion*, edited by Carolyn Saarni and Paul L. Harris. New York: Cambridge University Press.

Gouldner, Alvin W. 1973. *For Sociology: Renewal and Critique in Sociology Today*. New York: Basic Books.

Grandey, Alicia A., James M. Diefendorff, and Deborah E. Rupp. 2013. *Emotional Labor in the 21st Century: Diverse Perspectives on Emotion Regulation at Work*. New York: Routledge.

Grills, Scott. 2020. "Understanding Everyday Life: Generic Social Processes and the Pursuit of Transcontextuality." *Symbolic Interaction* 43(4):615–636. https://doi.org/10.1002/symb.468.

Groggel, Anne. 2023. "'Horrible Slime Stories' When Serving Victims: The Labor of Role-taking and Secondary Trauma Exposure." *Qualitative Sociology* 46:47–76. https://doi.org/10.1007/s11133-022-09528-0

Gubrium, Jaber F. 1989. "Emotion Work and Emotive Discourse in the Alzheimer's Disease Experience." Pp. 243–268 in *Current Perspectives on Aging and the Life Cycle*, edited by David Unruh and Gail S. Livings. Greenwich, CT: JAI.

Gubrium, Jaber F. 1992. *Out of Control: Family Therapy and Domestic Disorder*. Newbury Park, CA: Sage.

Gubrium, Jaber F. and James A. Holstein. 1990. *What Is Family?* Mountain View, CA: Mayfield.

Gubrium, Jaber F. and James A. Holstein. 2009. "The Everyday Work and Auspices of Authenticity." Pp. 121–138 in *Authenticity in Culture, Self, and Society*, edited by Phil Vannini and Patrick Williams. Farnham: Ashgate.

Guy, Mary Ellen and Meredith A. Newman. 2004. "Women's Jobs, Men's Jobs: Sex Segregation and Emotional Labor." *Public Administration Review* 64:289–298. https://doi.org/10.1111/j.1540-6210.2004.00373.x

Hallett, Tim. 2003. "Emotional Feedback and Amplification in Social Interaction." *Sociological Quarterly* 44(4):705–726. https://doi.org/10.1111/j.1533-8525.2003.tb00532.x

Harlow, Roxanna 2003. "'Race Doesn't Matter, but…': The Effect of Race on Professors' Experiences and Emotion Management in the Undergraduate College Classroom." *Social Psychology Quarterly* 66(4):348–363. https://doi.org/10.2307/1519834

Harré, Rom. 1992. "The Discursive Creation of Human Psychology." *Symbolic Interaction* 15(4):515–527. https://doi.org/10.1525/si.1992.15.4.515

Harré, Rom and Robert Finlay-Jones. 1986. "Emotion Talk across Times." Pp. 220–233 in *The Social Construction of Emotions*, edited by Rom Harré. Oxford: Blackwell.

Harris, Scott R. 1997. "Status Inequality and Close Relationships: An Integrative Typology of Bond-Saving Strategies." *Symbolic Interaction* 20(1):1–20. https://doi.org/10.1525/si.1997.20.1.1

Harris, Scott R. 2010. *What Is Constructionism? Navigating Its Use in Sociology*. Boulder, CO: Lynne Rienner.

Harris, Scott R. 2022. *How to Critique Journal Articles in the Social Sciences*. 2nd Ed. Long Grove, IL: Waveland Press.

Harris, Scott R. and Kerry O. Ferris. 2009. "How Does It Feel to Be a Star? Identifying Emotion on the Red Carpet." *Human Studies* 32(2):133–152. https://doi.org/10.1007/s10746-009-9113-5

Haski-Leventhal, Debbie. 2009. "Altruism and Volunteerism: The Perceptions of Altruism in Four Disciplines and Their Impact on the Study of Volunteerism." *Journal for the Theory of Social Behaviour* 39(3):271–299. https://doi.org/10.1111/j.1468-5914.2009.00405.x

Hatfield, Elaine. 2009. "Equity Theory." Pp. 535–537 in *Encyclopedia of Human Relationships*, edited by Harry T. Reis and Susan Sprecher. Thousand Oaks, CA: Sage.

Hatfield, Elaine, Richard L. Rapson, and Katherine Aumer-Ryan. 2008. "Social Justice in Love Relationships: Recent Developments." *Social Justice Research* 21:413–431. https://doi.org/10.1007/s11211-008-0080-1

Heelas, Paul. 1986. "Emotion Talk across Cultures." Pp. 234–266 in *The Social Construction of Emotions*, edited by Rom Harré. Oxford: Blackwell.

Hegtvedt, Karen A. and Christie L. Parris. 2014. "Emotions in Justice Processes." Pp. 103–125 in *Handbook of the Sociology of Emotions* (Vol. II), edited by Jan E. Stets and Jonathan H. Turner. New York: Springer.

Hochschild, Arlie Russell. 1979. "Emotion Work, Feeling Rules, and Social Structure." *American Journal of Sociology* 85(3):551–575. https://doi.org/10.1086/227049

Hochschild, Arlie Russell. 1983. *The Managed Heart: Commercialization of Human Feeling*. Berkeley, CA: University of California Press.

Hochschild, Arlie Russell. 2003. *The Commercialization of Intimate Life: Notes from Home and Work*. Berkeley, CA: University of California Press.

Hochschild, Arlie Russell. 2013. "Can Emotional Labor Be Fun?" Ch. 2 in *So How's the Family? And Other Essays*. Berkeley, CA: University of California Press.

Holstein, James A. and Jaber F. Gubrium. 1995. *The Active Interview*. Thousand Oaks, CA: Sage.

Holyfield, Lori and Lilian Jonas. 2003. "From River God to Research Grunt: Identity, Emotions, and the River Guide." *Symbolic Interaction* 26(2):285–306. https://doi.org/10.1525/si.2003.26.2.285

Homans, George C. 1958. "Social Behavior as Exchange." *American Journal of Sociology* 63:597–606. http://www.jstor.org/stable/2772990

Howard, Christina, Keith Tuffin, and Christine Stephens. 2000. "Unspeakable Emotion: A Discursive Analysis of Police Talk about Reactions to Trauma." *Journal of Language and Social Psychology* 19(3):295–314. https://doi.org/10.1177/0261 927X00019003

Humphrey, Ronald H. 2012. "How Do Leaders Use Emotional Labor?" *Journal of Organizational Behavior* 33:740–744. https://doi.org/10.1002/job.1791

Illouz, Eva. 2012. *Why Love Hurts: A Sociological Explanation*. Cambridge: Polity.

Izard, Carroll E. 2010. "The Many Meanings/Aspects of Emotion: Definitions, Functions, Activation, and Regulation." *Emotion Review* 2(4):363–370. https://doi.org/10.1177/1754073910374661

James, William. 1884. "What Is an Emotion?" *Mind* 9:188–205. https://doi.org/10.1093/mind/os-IX.34.188

Jackson, Brandon A. 2018. "Beyond the Cool Pose: Black Men and Emotion Management Strategies." *Sociology Compass* 12:1–14. https://doi.org/10.1111/soc4.12569

Jacobsen, Michael Hviid. 2023a. "Ambivalence: Exploring a Mixed Emotion." Ch. 14 in *Emotions in Culture and Everyday Life: Conceptual, Theoretical and Empirical Explorations*, edited by Michael Hviid Jacobsen. New York: Routledge.

Jacobsen, Michael Hviid. (editor). 2023b. *Emotions in Culture and Everyday Life: Conceptual, Theoretical and Empirical Explorations*. New York: Routledge.

Johnston, Erin F. 2021. "The Feeling of Enlightenment: Managing Emotions through Yoga and Prayer." *Symbolic Interaction* 44(3):576–602. https://doi.org/10.1002/symb.521

Kalat, James W. and Michelle N. Shiota. 2007. *Emotion*. Belmont, CA: Wadsworth.

Kang, Miliann. 2003. "The Managed Hand: The Commercialization of Bodies and Emotions in Korean Immigrant-Owned Nail Salons." *Gender & Society* 17(6):820–839. https://doi.org/10.1177/0891243203257632

Katz, Jack. 1988. *Seductions of Crime: Moral and Sensual Attractions of Doing Evil*. New York: Basic Books.

Kemper, Theodore D. 2000. "Social Models in the Explanation of Emotions." Pp. 45–58 in *Handbook of Emotions*, edited by Michael Lewis and Jeannette M. Haviland-Jones. New York: Guilford.

Kolb, Kenneth H. 2011. "Sympathy Work: Identity and Emotion Management among Victim Advocates and Counselors." *Qualitative Sociology* 34:101–119. https://doi.org/10.1007/s11133-010-9177-6

Kolb, Kenneth H. 2014a. "Emotional Subcultures." *Sociology Compass* 8(11):1229–1241. https://doi.org/10.1111/soc4.12207

Kolb, Kenneth H. 2014b. *Moral Wages: The Emotional Dilemmas of Victim Advocacy and Counseling*. Oakland, CA: University of California Press.

Konradi, Amanda. 1999. "'I Don't Have to Be Afraid of You': Rape Survivors' Emotion Management in Court." *Symbolic Interaction* 22(1):45–77. https://doi.org/10.1016/S0195-6086(99)80003-4

Kotchemidova, Christina. 2005. "From Good Cheer to 'Drive-by Smiling': A Social History of Cheerfulness." *Journal of Social History* 39(1):5–37. https://doi.org/10.1353/jsh.2005.0108

Kövecses, Zoltán. 2000. *Metaphor and Emotion: Language, Culture, and Body in Human Feeling*. New York: Cambridge University Press.

Kwate, Naa Oyo A. and Ilan H. Meyer. 2010. "The Myth of Meritocracy and African American Health." *American Journal of Public Health* 100(10):1831–1834. DOI: 10.2105/AJPH.2009.186445

Lakoff, George and Mark Johnson. 1980. *Metaphors We Live By*. Chicago: University of Chicago Press.

Lawler, Edward J. and Shane R. Thye. 1999. "Bringing Emotions into Social Exchange Theory." *Annual Review of Sociology* 25:217–244. https://doi.org/10.1146/annurev.soc.25.1.217

Leidner, Robin. 1993. *Fast Food, Fast Talk: The Routinization of Everyday Life*. Berkeley, CA: University of California Press.

Leidner, Robin. 1999. "Emotional Labor in Service Work." *Annals of the American Academy of Political and Social Science* 561:81–95. https://doi.org/10.1177/0002716299561001

Lerum, Kari. 2001. "'Precarious Situations' in a Strip Club: Exotic Dancers and the Problem of Reality Maintenance." Pp. 279–287 in *The Production of Reality* (3rd Ed.), edited by Jodi O'Brien and Peter Kollock. Thousand Oaks, CA: Pine Forge Press.

Lively, Kathryn J. 2006. "Emotions in the Workplace." Pp. 569–590 in *Handbook of the Sociology of Emotions*, edited by Jonathan H. Turner, and Jan E. Stets. New York: Springer.

Lively, Kathryn J. 2013. "Social and Cultural Influencers: Gender Effects on Emotional Labor at Work and at Home." Pp. 223–249 in *Emotional Labor in the 21st Century: Diverse Perspectives on Emotion Regulation at Work*, edited by Alicia A. Grandey, James M. Diefendorff, and Deborah E. Rupp. New York: Routledge.

Liu, Chien. 2003. "Does Quality of Marital Sex Decline with Duration?" *Archives of Sexual Behavior* 32(1):55–60. https://doi.org/10.1023/A:1021893329377

Locke, Abigail. 2003. "'If I'm Not Nervous, I'm Worried, Does that Make Sense?' The Use of Emotion Concepts by Athletes in Accounts of Performance." *Forum: Qualitative Social Research* 4(1). http://nbn-resolving.de/urn:nbn:de:0114-fqs0301105

Lofland, Lyn H. 1985. "The Social Shaping of Emotion: The Case of Grief." *Symbolic Interaction* 8:171–190. https://doi.org/10.1525/si.1985.8.2.171

Lois, Jennifer. 2001. "Managing Emotions, Intimacy, and Relationships in a Volunteer Search and Rescue Group." *Journal of Contemporary Ethnography* 30:131–179. https://doi.org/10.1177/089124101030002001

Lois, Jennifer. 2013. *Home Is Where the School Is: The Logic of Homeschooling and the Emotional Labor of Mothering*. New York: NYU Press.

Lois, Jennifer and Joanna Gregson. 2019. "Aspirational Emotion Work: Calling, Emotional Capital, and Becoming a 'Real' Writer." *Journal of Contemporary Ethnography* 48(1):51–79. https://doi.org/10.1177/0891241617749011

Lopez, Steven H. 2006. "Emotional Labor and Organized Emotional Care: Conceptualizing Nursing Home Care Work." *Work and Occupations* 33(2):133–160. https://doi.org/10.1177/0730888405284567

Loseke, Donileen R. 2009. "Examining Emotion as Discourse: Emotion Codes and Presidential Speeches Justifying War." *Sociological Quarterly* 50:497–524. https://doi.org/10.1111/j.1533-8525.2009.01150.x

Loseke, Donileen R. and Margarethe Kusenbach. 2008. "The Social Construction of Emotion." Pp. 511–529 in *Handbook of Constructionist Research*, edited by Jaber F. Gubrium, and James A. Holstein. New York: Guilford.

Lutz, Catherine A. 1988. *Unnatural Emotions: Everyday Sentiments on a Micronesian Atoll and their Challenges to Western Theory*. Chicago: University of Chicago Press.

Lutz, Catherine and Geoffrey M. White. 1986. "The Anthropology of Emotions." *Annual Review of Anthropology* 15:405–436. https://doi.org/10.1146/annurev.an.15.100186.002201

Martin, Patricia Yancey. 2005. *Rape Work: Victims, Gender, and Emotions in Organization and Community Context.* New York: Routledge.

Martin, Susan Ehrlich. 1999. "Police Force or Police Service? Gender and Emotional Labor." *Annals of the American Academy of Political and Social Science* 561:111–126. https://doi.org/10.1177/000271629956100108

Marwick, Alice and Nicole B. Ellison. 2012. "'There Isn't Wifi in Heaven!' Negotiating Visibility on Facebook Memorial Pages." *Journal of Broadcasting & Electronic Media* 56(3):378–400. https://doi.org/10.1080/08838151.2012.7.5197

Matt, Susan J. and Peter N. Stearns (eds.). 2014. *Doing Emotions History.* Chicago: University of Illinois Press.

Mayall, Berry. 1998. "Children, Emotions and Daily Life at Home and School." Pp. 135–154 in *Emotions and Social Life: Critical Themes and Contemporary Issues*, edited by Gillian Bendelow and Simon J. Williams. New York: Routledge.

McCarthy, E. Doyle. 1989. "Emotions Are Social Things: An Essay in the Sociology of Emotions." Pp. 51–72 in *The Sociology of Emotions: Original Essays and Research Papers*, edited by David D. Franks and E. Doyle McCarthy. Greenwich, CT: JAI.

McCarthy, E. Doyle. 2021. "Emotion and Culture: Interactionist Perspectives." Pp. 166–177 in *The Routledge International Handbook of Interactionism*, edited by Dirk vom Lehn, Natalia Ruiz-Junco, and Will Gibson. New York: Routledge.

McNamee, Stephen J. 2024. *The Meritocracy Myth.* 5th Ed. Lanham, MD: Rowman & Littlefield.

Meanwell, Emily, Joseph D. Wolfe, and Tim Hallett. 2008. "Old Paths and New Directions: Studying Emotions in the Workplace." *Sociology Compass* 2:537–559. https://doi.org/10.1111/j.1751-9020.2007.00077.x

Meanwell, Emily and Sibyl Kleiner. 2014. "The Emotional Experience of First-Time Teaching: Reflections from Graduate Instructors, 1997–2006." *Teaching Sociology* 42(1):17–27. https://doi.org/10.1177/0092055X1350837

Mears, Ashley and William Finley. 2005. "Not Just a Paper Doll: How Models Manage Bodily Capital and Why They Perform Emotional Labor." *Journal of Contemporary Ethnography* 34(3):317–343. https://doi.org/10.1177/0891241605274559

Mesquita, Batja and Ellen Delvaux. 2013. "A Cultural Perspective on Emotional Labor." Pp. 251–272 in *Emotional Labor in the 21st Century: Diverse Perspectives on Emotion Regulation at Work*, edited by Alicia A. Grandey, James M. Diefendorff, and Deborah E. Rupp. New York: Routledge.

Monahan, Brian A. 2010. *The Shock of the News: Media Coverage and the Making of 9/11.* New York: NYU Press.

Montemurro, Beth. 2002. "'You Go 'Cause You Have to': The Bridal Shower as a Ritual of Obligation." *Symbolic Interaction* 25(1):67–92. https://doi.org/10.1525/si.2002.25.1.67

Moon, Dawne. 2005. "Emotion Language and Social Power: Homosexuality and Narratives of Pain in Church." *Qualitative Sociology* 28(4):327–349. https://doi.org/10.1007/s11133-005-8362-5

Morris, Patricia. 2012. "Managing Pet Owners' Guilt and Grief in Veterinary Euthanasia Encounters." *Journal of Contemporary Ethnography* 41(3):337–365. https://doi.org/10.1177/0891241611435099

Musson, Gill and Katy Marsh. 2008. "Homeworking: Managing the Emotional Boundaries of Telework." Pp. 121–133 in *The Emotional Organization: Passions and Power*, edited by Stephen Fineman. Oxford: Blackwell.

Nelson, Margaret K. 2011. "Love and Gratitude: Single Mothers Talk about Men's Contributions to the Second Shift." Pp. 100–111 in *At the Heart of Work and Family: Engaging the Ideas of Arlie Hochschild*, edited by Anita Ilta Garey and Karen V. Hansen. New Brunswick, NJ: Rutgers.

Nelson, Timothy J. 1996. "Sacrifice of Praise: Emotion and Collective Participation in an African-American Worship Service." *Sociology of Religion* 57(4):379–396. https://doi.org/10.2307/3711893

Nestor, Mark S., Daniel L. Fischer, and David Arnold. 2020. "'Masking' our Emotions: Botulinum Toxin, Facial Expression, and Well-being in the Age of COVID-19." *Journal of Cosmetic Dermatology* 19:2154–2160. https://doi.org/10.1111/jocd.13569

Nomaguchi, Kei M. and Melissa A. Milkie. 2003. "Costs and Rewards of Children: The Effects of Becoming a Parent on Adults' Lives." *Journal of Marriage and Family* 65(2):356–374. https://doi.org/10.1111/j.1741-3737.2003.00356.x

Norgaard, Kari Marie. 2006. "'People Want to Protect Themselves a Little Bit': Emotions, Denial, and Social Movement Nonparticipation." *Sociological Inquiry* 76:372–396. https://doi.org/10.1111/j.1475-682X.2006.00160.x

Ortony, Andrew. 2022. "Are All 'Basic Emotions' Emotions? A Problem for the (Basic) Emotions Construct." *Perspectives on Psychological Science* 17(1):41–61. https://doi.org/10.1177/1745691620985415

Pearce, Jessica S. 2020. "Lafayette Strong: A Content Analysis of Grief and Support Online Following a Theater Shooting." *Illness, Crisis & Loss* 28(4):299–320. https://doi.org/10.1177/1054137317742234

Peterson, Gretchen. 2006. "Cultural Theory and Emotions." Pp. 114–134 in *Handbook of the Sociology of Emotions*, edited by Jonthan H. Turner and Jan E. Stets. New York: Springer.

Peterson, Gretchen. 2014. "Sports and Emotions." Pp. 495–510 in *Handbook of the Sociology of Emotions* (Vol. II), edited by Jan E. Stets and Jonathan H. Turner. New York: Springer.

Phillips, Scott W. 2016. "Police Discretion and Boredom: What Officers Do When There Is Nothing to Do." *Journal of Contemporary Ethnography* 45(5):580–601. https://doi.org/10.1177/0891241615587385

Pierce, Jennifer L. 1995. *Gender Trials: Emotional Lives in Contemporary Law Firms*. Berkeley: University of California Press.

Pierce, Jennifer L. 1999. "Emotional Labor among Paralegals." *Annals of the American Academy of Political and Social Science* 561:127–142. https://doi.org/10.1177/000271629956100109

Pogrebin, Mark R. and Eric D. Poole. 2003. "Humor in the Briefing Room: A Study of the Strategic Uses of Humor among Police." Pp. 80–93 in *Qualitative Approaches to Criminal Justice*, edited by Mark Pogrebin. Thousand Oaks, CA: Sage.

Pollak, Lauren Harte and Peggy A. Thoits. 1989. "Processes in Emotional Socialization." *Social Psychology Quarterly* 52:22–34. https://doi.org/10.2307/2786901

Prus, Robert C. 1989. *Making Sales: Influence as Interpersonal Accomplishment*. Newbury Park, CA: Sage.

Prus, Robert C. 1996. *Symbolic Interaction and Ethnographic Research: Intersubjectivity and the Study of Human Lived Experience*. Albany, NY: SUNY.

Rafaeli, Anat and Robert I. Sutton. 1991. "Emotional Contrast Strategies as Means of Social Influence: Lessons from Criminal Interrogators and Bill Collectors." *Academy of Management Journal* 34(4):749–775. https://doi.org/10.5465/256388

Ricketts, Thomas and Ann Macaskill. 2003. "Gambling as Emotion Management: Developing a Grounded Theory of Problem Gambling." *Addiction Research and Theory* 11(6):383–400. https://doi.org/10.1080/1606635031000062074

Rigney, Daniel. 2001. *The Metaphorical Society: An Invitation to Social Theory.* Lanham, MD: Rowman & Littlefield.

Rivera, Kendra Dyanne. 2015. "Emotional Taint: Making Sense of Emotional Dirty Work at the U.S. Border Patrol." *Management Communication Quarterly* 29(2):198–228. https://doi.org/10.1177/0893318914554090

Roberts, Alison and Keri Iyall Smith. 2002. "Managing Emotions in the College Classroom: The Cultural Diversity Course as an Example." *Teaching Sociology* 30(3):291–301. https://doi.org/10.2307/3211478

Rodriguez, Noelie and Alan Ryave. 2002. *Systematic Self-Observation.* Thousand Oaks, CA: Sage.

Rodriquez, Jason. 2011. "'It's a Dignity Thing': Nursing Home Care Workers' Use of Emotions." *Sociological Forum* 26(2):265–286. https://doi.org/10.1111/j.1573-7861.2011.01240.x

Rose, Mary R., Janice Nadler, and Jim Clark. 2006. "Appropriately Upset? Emotion Norms and Perceptions of Crime Victims." *Law and Human Behavior* 30(2):203–219. https://doi.org/10.1007/s10979-006-9030-3

Rosenberg, Morris. 1990. "Reflexivity and Emotions." *Social Psychology Quarterly* 53:3–12. https://doi.org/10.2307/2786865

Russell, James A. 1989. "Culture, Scripts, and Children's Understanding of Emotion." Pp. 293–318 in *Children's Understanding of Emotion*, edited by Carolyn Saarni and Paul L. Harris. New York: Cambridge University Press.

Russell, James A. 1991. "Culture and the Categorization of Emotions." *Psychological Bulletin* 110:426–450.

Sabra, Jakob Borrits. 2017. "'I Hate When They Do That!' Netiquette in Mourning and Memorialization among Danish Facebook Users." *Journal of Broadcasting & Electronic Media* 61(1):24–40. https://doi.org/10.1080/08838151.2016.1273931

Sallaz, Jeffrey J. 2002. "The House Rules: Autonomy and Interests among Service Workers in the Contemporary Casino Industry." *Work and Occupations* 29(4):394–427. https://doi.org/10.1177/0730888402029004002

Santin, Marlene and Benjamin Kelly. 2017. "The Managed Heart Revisited: Exploring the Effect of Institutional Norms on the Emotional Labor of Flight Attendants Post 9/11." *Journal of Contemporary Ethnography* 46(5):519–543. https://doi.org/10.1177/0891241615619991

Sarkisian, Natalia and Naomi Gerstel. 2012. *Nuclear Family Values, Extended Family Lives.* New York: Routledge.

Schachter, Stanley and Jerome E. Singer. 1962. "Cognitive, Social, and Physiological Determinants of Emotional State." *Psychological Review* 69:379–399.

Scheff, Thomas J. 1994. *Bloody Revenge: Emotions, Nationalism, and War.* Boulder, CO: Westview Press.

Scheff, Thomas J. 2016. "Depression, Bipolarity and Aggression as Emotion Sequences." *Journal of General Practice* 4(2):1–6.

Scheper-Hughes, Nancy. 1992. *Death without Weeping: The Violence of Everyday Life in Brazil.* Berkeley, CA: University of California.

Schrock, Douglas and Brian Knop. 2014. "Gender and Emotions." Pp. 411–428 in *Handbook of the Sociology of Emotions* (Vol. II), edited by Jan E. Stets and Jonathan H. Turner. New York: Springer.

Schwalbe, Michael, Sandra Godwin, Daphne Holden, Douglas Schrock, Shealy Thompson, and Michelle Wolkomir. 2000. "Generic Processes in the Reproduction of Inequality: An Interactionist Analysis." *Social Forces* 79:419–452. https://doi.org/10.2307/2675505

Schwarz, Ori. 2018. "Emotional Ear Drops: The Music Industry and Technologies of Emotional Management." Pp. 56–78 in *Emotions as Commodities: Capitalism, Consumption and Authenticity*, edited by Eva Illouz. New York: Routledge.

Schweingruber, David, Sine Anahita, and Nancy Berns. 2004. "'Popping the Question' when the Answer Is Known: The Engagement Proposal as Performance." *Sociological Focus* 37(2):143–161. https://doi.org/10.1080/00380237.2004.10571239

Schweingruber, David and Nancy Berns. 2005. "Shaping the Selves of Young Salespeople through Emotion Management." *Journal of Contemporary Ethnography* 34:679–706. https://doi.org/10.1177/0891241605280519

Scott, Marvin B. and Stanford M. Lyman. 1968. "Accounts." *American Sociological Review* 33:46–62. https://doi.org/10.2307/2092239

Scott, Clifton and Karen Kroman Myers. 2005. "The Socialization of Emotion: Learning Emotion Management at the Fire Station." *Journal of Applied Communication Research* 33(1):67–92. https://doi.org/10.1080/0090988042000318521

Sharp, Shane. 2010. "How Does Prayer Help Manage Emotions?" *Social Psychology Quarterly* 73(4):417–437. https://doi.org/10.1177/0190272510389129

Simon, Robin W., Donna Eder, and Cathy Evans. 1992. "The Development of Feeling Norms Underlying Romantic Love among Adolescent Females." *Social Psychology Quarterly* 55:29–46. https://doi.org/10.2307/2786684

Simonova, Olga. 2017. "Emotion Management and the Professional Culture of Administrative Social Workers in Russia: Common Standards Versus the Moral Mission of Social Care." *The Journal of Social Policy Studies* 15(1):129–142.

Sinden, Jane Lee. 2010. "The Normalization of Emotion and the Disregard of Health Problems in Elite Amateur Sport." *Journal of Clinical Sport Psychology* 4:241–256. https://doi.org/10.1123/jcsp.4.3.241

Smith, Allen C. III and Sherryl Kleinman. 1989. "Managing Emotions in Medical School." *Social Psychology Quarterly* 52:56–69. https://doi.org/10.2307/2786904

Snyder, Eldon E. 1990. "Emotion and Sport: A Case Study of Collegiate Women Gymnasts." *Sociology of Sport Journal* 7:254–270. https://doi.org/10.1123/ssj.7.3.254

Snyder, Eldon E. and Ronald Ammons. 1993. "Baseball's Emotion Work: Getting Psyched to Play." *Qualitative Sociology* 16:111–132. https://doi.org/10.1007/BF00989746

Stanton, Andrea L. 2014. "Islamic Emoticons: Pious Sociability and Community Building in Online Muslim Communities." Pp. 80–98 in *Internet and Emotions*, edited by Tova Benski and Eran Fisher. New York: Routledge.

Staske, Shirley A. 1996. "Talking Feelings: The Collaborative Construction of Emotion in Talk between Close Relational Partners." *Symbolic Interaction* 19:111–135. https://doi.org/10.1525/si.1996.19.2.111

Stein, Michael. 1989. "Gratitude and Attitude: A Note on Emotional Welfare." *Social Psychology Quarterly* 52(3):242–248. https://doi.org/10.2307/2786719

Stenross, Barbara and Sherryl Kleinman. 1989. "The Highs and Lows of Emotional Labor: Detectives Encounters with Criminals and Victims." *Journal of Contemporary Ethnography* 17:435–452. https://doi.org/10.1177/089124189017004003

Stets, Jan E. and Ryan Trettevik. 2014. "Emotions in Identity Theory." Pp. 33–49 in *Handbook of the Sociology of Emotions* (Vol. II), edited by Jan E. Stets and Jonathan H. Turner. New York: Springer.

Stets, Jan E. and Jonathan H. Turner (eds.). 2014. *Handbook of the Sociology of Emotions* (Vol. II). New York: Springer.

Stockard, Janice E. 2002. *Marriage in Culture: Practice and Meaning across Diverse Societies.* New York: Harcourt.

Surma, Jerzy. 2016. "Social Exchange in Online Social Networks: The Reciprocity Phenomenon on Facebook." *Computer Communications* 73:342–346. https://doi.org/10.1016/j.comcom.2015.06.017

Taylor, Lou. 2009. *Mourning Dress: A Costume and Social History.* New York: Routledge.

Thoits, Peggy A. 1985. "Self-Labeling Processes in Mental Illness: The Role of Emotional Deviance." *American Journal of Sociology* 91:221–249. https://doi.org/10.1086/228276

Thoits, Peggy A. 1990. "Emotional Deviance: Research Agendas." Pp. 180–203 in *Research Agendas in the Sociology of Emotions*, edited by Theodore D. Kemper. Albany, NY: SUNY.

Thoits, Peggy A. 1996. "Managing the Emotions of Others." *Symbolic Interaction* 19:85–109. https://doi.org/10.1525/si.1996.19.2.85

Thoits, Peggy A. 2004. "Emotion Norms, Emotion Work, and Social Order." Pp. 359–378 in *Feelings and Emotions: The Amsterdam Symposium*, edited by Antony S. R. Manstead, Nico Frijda, and Agneta Fischer. New York: Cambridge University Press.

Tian, Xiaoli and Yanan Guo. 2021. "An Online Acquaintance Community: The Emergence of Chinese Virtual Civility." *Symbolic Interaction* 44(4):771–797. https://doi.org/10.1002/symb.537

Tracy, Sarah J. 2005. "Locking Up Emotion: Moving Beyond Dissonance for Understanding Emotion Labor Discomfort." *Communication Monographs* 72:261–283. https://doi.org/10.1080/03637750500206474

Tracy, Sarah J. and Karen Tracy 1998. "Emotion Labor at 911: A Case Study and Theoretical Critique." *Journal of Applied Communication Research* 26:390–411. https://doi.org/10.1080/00909889809365516

Turner, Jonthan H. 2011. *The Problem of Emotions in Societies.* New York: Routledge.

Turner, Jonathan H. 2022. "Why Are Humans So Emotional? An Analysis from Evolutionary Sociology." Ch. 3 in *The Oxford Handbook of Emotional Development*, edited by Daniel Dukes, Eric Walle, and Andrea Samson. Oxford, UK: Oxford University Press.

Turner, Jonathan H. and Jan E. Stets. 2005. *The Sociology of Emotions.* New York: Cambridge University Press.

Turner, Ronny E., Charles Edgley, and Glen Olmstead. 1975. "Information Control in Conversations: Honesty Is Not Always the Best Policy." *Kansas Journal of Sociology* 11(1):69–89. https://www.jstor.org/stable/23255229

van Brakel, Jaap. 1994. "Emotions: A Cross-Cultural Perspective on Forms of Life." Pp. 179–237 in *Social Perspectives on Emotion* (Vol. II), edited by William M. Wentworth and John Ryan. Greenwich, CT: JAI.

van Jaarsveld, Danielle and Winnie R. Poster. 2013. "Call Centers: Emotional Labor over the Phone." Pp. 153–173 in *Emotional Labor in the 21st Century: Diverse Perspectives on Emotion Regulation at Work*, edited by Alicia A. Grandey, James M. Diefendorff, and Deborah E. Rupp. New York: Routledge.

Wallace, Anthony F. C. and Margaret T. Carson. 1973. "Sharing and Diversity in Emotion Terminology." *Ethos* 1(1):1–29.

Waller, Willard. 1937. "The Rating and Dating Complex." *American Sociological Review* 2(5):727–734. https://doi.org/10.2307/2083825

Walster, Elaine, G. William Walster, and Ellen Berscheid. 1978. *Equity: Theory and Research*. Boston: Allyn and Bacon.

Ward, Jenna and Robert McMurray. 2016. *The Dark Side of Emotional Labor*. New York: Routledge.

Wells, Alan. 1990. "Popular Music: Emotional Use and Management." *Journal of Popular Culture* 24(1):105–117. https://doi.org/10.1111/j.0022-3840.1990.00105.x

Whalen, Jack and Don H. Zimmerman. 1998. "Observations on the Display and Management of Emotion in Naturally Occurring Activities: The Case of 'Hysteria' in Calls to 9-1-1." *Social Psychology Quarterly* 61:141–159. https://doi.org/10.2307/2787066

Wharton, Amy S. 2009. "The Sociology of Emotional Labor." *Annual Review of Sociology* 35:147–165. https://doi.org/10.1146/annurev-soc-070308-115944

Wierzbicka, Anna. 1999. *Emotions across Languages and Cultures: Diversity and Universals*. Cambridge: Cambridge University Press.

Wilkins, Amy C. 2008. "'Happier than Non-Christians': Collective Emotions and Symbolic Boundaries among Evangelical Christians." *Social Psychology Quarterly* 71:281–301. https://doi.org/10.1177/019027250807100308

Williams, Apryl A., Zaida Bryant, Christopher Carvell. 2019. "Uncompensated Emotional Labor, Racial Battle Fatigue, and (In)Civility in Digital Spaces." *Sociology Compass* 13(2):e12658. https://doi.org/10.1111/soc4.12658

Wilson, John. 2000. "Volunteering." *Annual Review of Sociology* 26:215–240. https://doi.org/10.1146/annurev.soc.26.1.215

Wingfield, Adia Harvey. 2010. "Are Some Emotions Marked 'Whites Only'? Racialized Feeling Rules in Professional Workplaces." *Social Problems* 57:251–268. https://doi.org/10.1525/sp.2010.57.2.251

Wingfield, Adia Harvey. 2021. "The (Un)Managed Heart: Racial Contours of Emotion Work in Gendered Occupations." *Annual Review of Sociology* 47:197–212. https://doi.org/10.1146/annurev-soc-081320-114850

Witz, Anne, Chris Warhurst, and Dennis Nickson. 2003. "The Labour of Aesthetics and the Aesthetics of Organization." *Organization* 10(1):33–54. https://doi.org/10.1177/1350508403010001375

Wolkomir, Michelle. 2001. "Emotion Work, Commitment, and the Authentication of the Self: The Case of Gay and Ex-Gay Christian Support Groups." *Journal of Contemporary Ethnography* 30:305–334. https://doi.org/10.1177/089124101030003002

Wolkomir, Michelle and Jennifer Powers. 2007. "Helping Women and Protecting the Self: The Challenge of Emotional Labor in an Abortion Clinic." *Qualitative Sociology* 30:153–169. https://doi.org/10.1007/s11133-006-9056-3

Yeomans, Liz. 2019. *Public Relations as Emotional Labour*. New York: Routledge.

Zuckerman, Phil. 2008. *Society without God: What the Least Religious Nations Can Tell Us about Contentment.* New York: NYU Press.

Zurcher, Louis A. 1970. "The 'Friendly' Poker Game: A Study of an Ephemeral Role." *Social Forces* 49(2):173–186. https://doi.org/10.2307/2576518

Zurcher, Louis A. 1982. "The Staging of Emotion: A Dramaturgical Analysis." *Symbolic Interaction* 5:1–22. https://doi.org/10.1525/si.1982.5.1.1

Index

accidie 85
Adler, Patricia 36
Adler, Peter 36
advertising 65–6
Albas, Cheryl 21, 24, 26, 36–8, 40, 103
Albas, Daniel 21, 24, 26, 36–8, 40, 103
aloha 98
Al-Shawaf, Laith 3
altruism 50–1
amae 84
ambiguity, physiological 82–4
ambivalence 11, 21, 45, 56–8, 73, 76
American Idol 7–8
Ammons, Ronald 37, 40
Anahita, Sine 18
Arcy, Jacquelyn 50
Arluke, Arnold 80
Arnold, David 34
Ash, Mary K. 38
Ashkanasy, Neal M. 65, 77
Aumer-Ryan, Katherine 52
Averill, James R. 84, 85, 99

Bachen, Christine M. 18, 24
Bareither, Christoph 9, 97
Barrett, Lisa Feldman 82
Bellas, Marcia L. 23, 26, 32, 61, 68–9
beneficence, principle of 50–1
Berger, Peter xi 15, 17, 102
Berns, Nancy 18, 25, 64, 66–8, 74, 76, 99
Berscheid, Ellen 51
Best, Joel 99
bill collectors 40, 42, 80, 103
biology 3–4, 10–11, 82–4, 87
Blau, Peter M. 49, 59
Bloch, Charlotte 79
Blumer, Herbert 50
bodily ambiguity 82–4

bodily deep acting 36–8, 41–2, 103
bodily gestures 34, 94
border patrol 33, 75
boredom 32–3, 60–1, 85
Bos, Arjan E. R. 35
Briggs, Jean L. 11
Brownlie, Julie 25
Bryant, Zaida 23
burnout 11, 72–3, 76
Bush, George W. 30

Cain, Susan 57
Cahill, Spencer E. 47, 75
Cara, Alessia 83
Carson, Margaret T. 84
Carvell, Christopher 23
Casioppo, Danielle 84
Chagga 86, 99
Chandler, Amy 36
Chavez, Sergio 69
Chewong 84
Christianity 43–4, 100
Clanton, Gordon 10, 14, 18–19
Clark, Candace xi, 2, 3, 5, 50–1, 55–6, 58, 84–5, 106
Clark, Jim 15
closure 25, 85, 99
clothing 16–17, 21, 34–5, 63
cognitive deep acting 6, 11, 36, 38–41, 44, 53–4, 58, 63–4, 67, 73, 81, 97, 102
cognitive labor 60
Collins, Randall 106
complementarity, principle of 50–1
compliments 17, 49, 61, 95
Copp, Martha 64
Cottingham, Marci D. 22, 71
Coupland, Christine 18, 88, 90
Covid-19 33

124 Index

Crabtree, Arialle K. 15
critical thinking 77, 104
crying 82
cynicism 73–4, 76

Danesi, Marce l94
Daus, Catherine S. 65, 77
Davis, Joseph E. 14, 21
death 10, 20, 25, 27–8, 40, 74–5, 85, 88
declining marginal utility (DMU) 49
deep acting 4–6, 11, 36–46, 53–4, 58, 60–4, 67, 73–6, 81, 97, 102–4, 106
definitions: deep acting 4, 36; emotion 10–11; emotion management 31; emotion norms 13; emotional labor 60–1; surface acting 4, 31; upgrading and downgrading emotion labels 91
Delaney, Kevin J. 16, 39, 61
Del Rosso, Jared 24, 29
Delvaux, Ellen 75
denial 93
Denmark 26–8
Derks, Daantje 35, 85
Derné, Steve 20, 29–30
Deshotels, Tina 79
Deutsch, Francine M. 22
Devault, Marjorie L. 69
DeWise, Lee 7–8
Diefendorff, James M. 78, 80
direct socialization 16–18, 63–4
disgust 8, 13, 33–4, 39, 85
displacement 94
Dixon, Thomas 11–12, 85
duration (too long or too short) 24–7

Edelblute, Heather 69
Eder, Donna 15
Edgley, Charles 89
Edwards, Derek 88
Eggleston, Robin 47
Eilish, Billie 6
Ellis, Carolyn 55
Ellis, Colter 39
Emanatian, Michele 86, 99
Emerson, Joan P. 21, 35
emojis 9, 85, 94–8, 100
emoticons 35, 85, 94
emotional labor: defined 60–1; advertising 65–6; drawbacks/benefits 72–7; emotional capital 74–5; gender 68–70; hiring 62–3; labeling emotions 97–8; monitoring/evaluating 64–5; race 70–1; status 71–2; training 63–4

emotion: automatic 4–5; basic 11; definitions 10–11; indescribable 7–9; irrational 5–6; psychological 9; private 6–7; biological dimensions 3–4, 82–4; trivial 1–2
emotion management: defined 31; deep acting 36–41; dishonest 44–5; interpersonal 41–3; prayer 43–4; surface acting 32–6
emotion norms: defined 13; debate/conflict 20–1; deviance 23–6; enforcement/sanctions 15–16, 64–5; exchange theory 54; inequality 22–3, 68–72; learning/socialization 16–18, 63–4; pervasive/invisible 14; variations/changes 18
Enarson, Elaine 60
English 84–7
envy 14–15, 39, 61, 85
Erickson, Rebecca J. 22, 61
Esala, Jennifer J. 24, 29
Evans, Cathy 15
Evans, Louwanda 70–1
Evans, Vyvyan 94–8
evolutionary theory 3, 101
exchange theory: defined 48–51; ambivalence 57–8; opportunity cost 49; declining marginal utility 49–50; four connections with emotions 51–5; misgivings 56–8; principle of beneficence 50–1; principle of complementarity 50–1; principle of reciprocity 50–1; sympathy 55–6
expressive deep acting 37–8

Facebook 26–8
facial expressions 33–4
fago 84
Feagin, Joe R. 70
fear 3, 8, 10, 33, 40–3, 61, 67, 81–2, 97, 99
Ferris, Kerry O. 8, 89–90, 100
Fine, Gary Alan 35
Finlay-Jones, Robert 85
Finley, William 80
Fischer, Agneta H. 35
Fischer, Daniel L. 34
Flower, Lisa 33
Forsyth, Craig J. 79
Francis, Linda E. 40
Franks, David 85, 101
Froyum, Carissa M. 47
funerals 3, 28, 35, 38, 40, 75
Furedi, Frank 99

Gallmeier, Charles P. 38, 42
gender 5–6, 16, 22–3, 59, 68–70, 87
German 84
Gerstel, Naomi 69
GIFs 9, 85
God 18, 39, 43–4
Goddard, Cliff 85
Goffman, Erving 13, 31, 43, 47
Goodrum, Sarah 25, 71, 103
Gordon, Steven L. 29
Gouldner, Alvin W. 58
Grandey, Alicia A. 78, 80
gratitude 2, 6, 14, 16, 20, 25, 31–5, 42, 45, 49, 51, 53–4, 57–9, 63, 84, 105
Gregson, Joanna 75
grief (mourning) 20, 25–8, 35
Grills, Scott 102
Groggel, Anne 79
Grove, Wendy J. C. 61
Gubrium, Jaber F. 22, 83, 92–3, 98
Guo, Yanan 26
Guy, Mary Ellen 68

Haapio-Kirk, Laura 100
Hallett, Tim 45, 60, 74, 80
happiness 8, 15, 24, 26, 35, 37, 39, 41, 52, 61, 64–5, 70, 74, 76, 79, 82–3, 87, 88–9, 95–7, 100, 102
Harlow, Roxanna 70
Harré, Rom 84–5, 88
Harris, Scott R. 8, 10–11, 26, 40–2, 46, 78, 89–90, 97, 100, 103
Haski-Leventhal, Debbie 50
hate 8, 91, 94
Hatfield, Elaine 49, 52
Heelas, Paul 8, 84–5
Hegtvedt, Karen A. 51, 59
Hochschild, Arlie R. viii, 1, 4, 6, 10–11, 14, 16, 24–5, 27, 29, 31, 36–7, 40–2, 46, 53–5, 57, 59, 62–3, 65–6, 69, 71–3, 75, 77, 80, 87–8, 97, 103
Holiday, Billie 83
Holstein, James A. 30, 83, 92–3
Holyfield, Lori 41, 80
Homans, George C. 49
Howard, Christina 18
Hozier 83
Hudson, Jennifer 8
Humphrey, Ronald H. 61

identifying emotions: defined 81; bodily ambiguity 82–4; celebrities 100; emojis 94–7; impression management 88–90; interactional coaching 90–1; interpersonal 90–2; labor 97–8; metaphors 86–7; perspectives on situations 87–8; upgrading and downgrading emotion labels 91–2; vocabularies 84–5; who knows best what someone is feeling 92–4
Ifaluk 84
Illongot 85
Illouz, Eva 18, 24, 59
imagined interaction 43–4, 67
indirect socialization 16–18, 63–4
inequality 22–3, 68–72, 77, 106
Instagram 35, 49
intensity (too much or too little) 24, 27
interactional coaching 90–1
isin 85
Irvine, Leslie 39

Jackson, Brandon A. 70
Jacobsen, Michael H. 21, 45, 57, 101
James, William 3
Japanese 84–6, 94
Javanese 85
Johnson, Dwayne "The Rock" 49
Johnson, Mark 87
Johnston, Erin F. 37
Jonas, Lilian 41, 80

Kalat, James W. 10, 12, 93
Kang, Miliann 79
Katz, Jack 2, 35
Kelly, Benjamin 75
Kemper, Theodore 46
Kleiner, Sibyl 26
Kleinman, Sherryl 33, 40, 73–4, 76, 105
Knop, Brian 22
Kolb, Kenneth H. 76, 103
Konradi, Amanda 21, 103
Kotchemidova, Christina 29, 62
Kövecses, Zoltán 86, 99, 100
Kusenbach, Margarethe 30
Kwate, Naa Oyo A. 23

Lakoff, George 87
Lawler, Edward J. 51, 59
Lawrence, Jennifer 71
Leidner, Robin 42, 60, 62–4, 79
Lerum, Kari 21
Lewis, David M. G. 3
Liu, Chien 49
Lively, Kathryn J. 72, 80
Locke, Abigail 90
Lofland, Lyn H. 20
Lois, Jennifer 24, 41, 47, 75

Lopez, Steven H. 74
Loseke, Donileen 2, 21, 23, 30
love 3, 7–8, 19, 29–30, 32, 35, 50–1, 59, 83–4, 90–3, 96, 99, 102, 104
Lyman, Stanford M. 39
lust 35, 85–6, 89, 99
Lutz, Catherine A. 84

Macaskill, Ann 40
Marsh, Katy 61
Martin, Patricia Yancey 34, 105
Martin, Susan Ehrlich 69
Matt, Susan J. 18
Mayall, Berry 22
McCarthy, E. Doyle 7
McMurray, Robert 18, 33, 74–5
McNamee, Stephen J. 22–3
Meanwell, Emily 26, 80
Mears, Ashley 80
melancholy 85
Mesquita, Batja 75
metaphors 30, 47, 86–7, 99–100
Meyer, Ilan H. 23
Milkie, Melissa A. 50
misgivings 56–8
Monahan, Brian A. 75
Montemurro, Beth 24
Moon, Dawne 22
Moore, Wendy L. 71
Morris, Patricia 41
Musson, Gill 61
Myers, Karen Kroman 62, 64, 79

n-adic interaction 26–7
Nadler, Janice 15
Nelson, Margaret K. 58–9
Nelson, Timothy J. 34
Nestor, Mark S. 34
Newman, Meredith A. 68
Nomaguchi, Kei M. 50
Norgaard, Kari Marie 40

Olmstead, Glen 89
opportunity cost 49, 53, 59
organizational shields 22, 71
Ortony, Andrew 10–11

Paige, Robin 69
Parris, Christie L. 51, 59
Pearce, Jessica S. 35, 47
Peterson, Gretchen 18, 37
Petty, Tom 6
Phillips, Scott W. 105

physical labor 60
Pierce, Jennifer L. 55, 69, 79
placing (wrong audience or arena) 25–7
Pogrebin, Mark R. 40
policing, interactional 15, 30
Pollak, Lauren Harte 84
Poole, Eric D. 40
Poster, Winnie R. 65
Powers, Jennifer 80
President Zelensky 8
pride 2, 10, 26, 35, 42, 53, 83–4, 98
privileged access 6–7, 92–3
projection 93–4
Prus, Robert C. 60, 102
psychoanalysis 93–4, 101
psychology 9, 12, 82, 93–4

Rafaeli, Anat 42
Rapson, Richard L. 52
rational hedonist 48, 50
rationality 5–6
reasons to study the sociology of emotions 77–8, 101–6
reciprocal beneficence 51
reciprocal complementarity 51
reciprocity 50–1
Richards, Patricia 15
Ricketts, Thomas 40
Rigney, Daniel 13, 22, 30, 48–9, 56, 59
Rivera, Kendra Dyanne 33, 75
road rage 85, 99
Roberts, Alison 32
Rodriguez, Noelie 45
Rodriquez, Jason 68, 74
Rose, Mary R. 15
Rosenberg, Morris 82–3
rule reminders 14
Rupp, Deborah E. 78, 80
Russell, James A. 8, 85
Ryave, Alan 45

Sabra, Jakob Borrits 26–8
Sallaz, Jeffrey J. 60, 63, 79
Samoans 8
Santin, Marlene 75
Sarkisian, Natalia 69
Schachter, Stanley 82
Scheff, Thomas J. 2, 101
Scheper-Hughes, Nancy 20
Schrock, Douglas 22
Schwalbe, Michael 23, 106
Schwarz, Ori 41

Schweingruber, David 18, 24, 64, 66–7, 74, 76
schwing 85, 99
Scott, Clifton 79
Scott, Marvin B. 39
Seacrest, Ryan 8
Sharp, Shane 43–4, 67, 100
Shaw, Frances 25
Shiota, Michelle N. 10, 12, 93
shock absorbers 66
Simon, Robin W. 15, 21
Simonova, Olga 61
Sinden, Jane Lee 18
Singer, Jerome E. 82
Smith, Allen C. 33, 40, 73–4, 76
Smith, Keri Iyall 32
Snyder, Eldon E. 37, 40
social norms 5, 13–16
socialization 16–18
society as legal order 30
society as market 59
society as theatre 47
Spock 5
spontaneity 45
Stafford, Mark C. 71
Stanton, Andrea L. 85
Star Trek 5
Staske, Shirley A. 91
status shields 23, 71–2, 103
Stearns, Peter N. 18
Stein, Michael 51
Stenross, Barbara 79, 105
Stevens, Christine 18
Stets, Jan E. ix, 11, 101
Stockard, Janice E. 20
surface acting 4, 31–6, 38, 42, 44–6, 57, 60, 63–4, 73, 78, 90, 96–8, 100, 102
Surma, Jerzy 50
Sutton, Robert I. 42
sympathy 6, 8, 25, 55–6, 61, 69, 89–90, 102

Taiwanese 84
Taylor, Lou 35

Thoits, Peggy A. 3, 13, 16, 21, 37–8, 40, 84, 97
Thye, Shane R. 51, 59
Tian, Xiaoli 26
TikTok 2, 26, 40
timing (too early or too late) 25
tone of voice 3, 4, 14–15, 17, 24, 32–3, 94–5
Tracy, Karen 32–3
Tracy, Sarah J. 32–3, 75–6, 80
Tuffin, Keith 18
Turner, Jonathan H. ix, 3, 11, 101
Turner, Ronny E. 89–90
Twitter 26, 28, 49, 71

Utku 8, 11

van Brakel, Jaap 10–11
van Jaarsveld, Danielle 65

Wallace, Anthony F. C. 84
Waller, Willard 49
Walster, Elaine 51
Walster, G. William 51
Wang, Xinyuan 100
Ward, Jenna 18, 33, 74–5
Wells, Alan 41
Whalen, Jack 98
Wharton, Amy S. 79–80
Wierzbicka, Anna 86
Wilkins, Amy C. 88, 100
Williams, Apryl A. 23, 71
Wilson, John 50
Wingfield, Adia Harvey 23, 70
Witz, Anne 63
Wolfe, Joseph D. 80
Wolkomir, Michelle 47, 80

Yeomans, Liz 79

Zimmerman, Don H. 98
Zuckerman, Phil 28
Zulu 86, 96
Zurcher, Louis A. 18, 33, 42

Made in the USA
Las Vegas, NV
07 February 2024

85470495R00079